SEEING THE
BLIND SPOT

SEEING THE
BLIND
SPOT

**PETER BLOOM
MARIANA MARTINEZ**

Copyright © 2019 by Peter Bloom and Mariana Martinez.

All rights reserved. No portions of this publication may be reproduced, distributed, transmitted, stored, performed, displayed, adapted or used in any form or manner without prior written permission, except for certain limited non-commercial uses permitted by the United States Copyright Act, such as brief quotations embodied in critical reviews.

Paperback ISBN: 9781075594083

Cover and Interior Design: Creative Publishing Book Design

CONTENTS

Preface   vii

Introduction   1

Chapter 1: Overlooking Family Relationships that Created an Impasse   7

Chapter 2: An Asset Distribution Plan that Produced Family Acrimony   29

Chapter 3: A Change of Direction at the Edge of the Cliff   49

Chapter 4: Business Problems and Family Problems Intertwined   77

Chapter 5: The Science Behind the Analysis: Bowen Family Systems Theory   109

PREFACE

Presentation

We are Mariana and Peter, colleagues who came to the field of family enterprise from different disciplines. Mariana is a psychologist with a specialty in family systems; Peter is a lawyer whose practice focuses on family businesses. We believe that having financial resources represents an advantage in life. We also know that without sound family relationships, wealth has limited benefits and does not endure across generations. With this in mind, we had extensive conversations about how our professional niches intersect when it comes to serving families about their financial legacy or family business. As a result of these conversations, we have enriched and expanded our perspectives about what represents best practices and what yields the most benefits to these families. Our exchanges became so meaningful that we decided to share our learning with other professionals who serve families of wealth, and with members of families interested in preserving their wealth and their family stability and cohesion.

The Author's Journeys that Led to this Book

From Peter Bloom

For many years, I delivered professional services to family businesses much like many colleagues who likewise worked with family business clients. My colleagues and I prepared succession plans and estate plans, created family councils and other governance structures, and helped families address other common challenges that arose in their businesses. Generally, the quality of the services that colleagues delivered was extraordinarily high, meaning that those services were technically proficient, sound in law, and sophisticated. The professionals who delivered these services were skilled, experienced, serious, and well-meaning. It is no exaggeration to say that as a group, these professionals represent the best of the best. Yet, as time passed and events unfolded, the intended and expected results from those services did not materialize: much of the work failed to achieve what, in retrospect, were the true objectives of clients. How could this be? What had happened?

The search for the answers to these questions became a years-long project that resulted in my reorientation as a professional. I moved toward a more holistic approach to the problems I was asked to address. I brought with me a greater awareness of the roles that family history, culture, relationships, individual personalities, and related factors played in outcomes. I may have been retained as a lawyer to help a family member or a family with a business problem, but it became evident that I was dealing with a *family* business problem. The solution to this type of problem always had to be grounded in the realization that those problems are always fundamentally different than problems among non-family members who were in business together in some way.

As a consequence of my search, I had to acknowledge that my own professional training could sometimes operate as an obstacle to achieving better outcomes for the families in my practice. The training any professional receives is very powerful, but by its nature, is highly focused. It can be limiting. It can discourage those of us who were not trained in behavioral sciences from considering—and prompting our clients to consider—the impact of family history, culture, and those other factors. And there is little professional incentive to do so: no one could ever reasonably accuse a lawyer of malpractice for proceeding simply as a client directs in a technically proficient and competent manner, without exploring those other issues.

But decades of working with family businesses tells me that unless those other issues are explored, the odds that a professional engagement will be ultimately successful are not high. The landmines are everywhere. It may be that a client does not accurately identify their own objectives. It might be that people find it difficult to explore some areas of their family life. For reasons rooted in their own personal history or personality, a client may not perceptively understand how their actions will dynamically impact the actions and responses of others in the family. These are vulnerabilities that represent some of the most serious threats to the achievement of the client's own stated objectives.

From Mariana Martinez

I have been fascinated by the extent by which family systems theory is useful in the field of family enterprise, family business, and legacy planning. I have been studying families for more than two decades, learning about what moves families, what "rules" govern their life and rhythms, and what issues impact the family functioning. Psychology and family dynamics have been my passion.

Some years ago, I was having a conversation with a lawyer (not my co-author) whose practice involved structuring family businesses and developing estate plans for high and ultra-high net worth families. He shared with me his frustration when he saw that often he worked with families developing sophisticated structures that were perfectly sound from the legal, tax, and financial point of view, but that were difficult or impossible for the families to implement, and detrimental to family relationships. It dawned on me that he must widen his lens to consider the emotional and relationship factors that were obstructing his best practice. He described families with individuals that were not ill-willed or incapable, but simply moved by the powerful undercurrents that governed family interactions. These families were up against the forces of emotionality that moves us all, but for them, failing to manage them constructively resulted in dire loss at the financial, personal, and family levels.

I decided to share what I knew about families with advisors that, up to that point, were far from my professional reach. I found that financial advisors, accountants, wealth managers, tax specialists, trustees, and other professionals working with families in businesses and families of wealth found these ideas valuable. I also found that enterprise families themselves benefited from learning about the way families function. Advisors acquired a way of thinking—systems thinking—that changed their approach to their clients, increasing

Preface

their chances of success. Families found a roadmap that guided their approach to practical problems. As my lawyer friend expressed, "knowing about family systems and addressing emotions and family relationships is a way to avoid the family issue land mines that are in the road of performing my work."

I hope this book ignites the curiosity of the readers and serves as motivation to expand their knowledge of family systems. I hope that they experience the excitement of looking at families from a new perspective.

INTRODUCTION

Families in business and families of wealth approach professionals to find solutions to financial and similar problems that arise. These professionals are expected to provide guidance in their area of expertise, but regardless of their particular field, they have to manage the emotions and family dynamics that are intertwined with every practical decision a family makes. Yet, professionals such as accountants, bankers, lawyers, trustees, and financial managers seldom receive training to do so. Issues such as perception of fairness, disappointment, family secrets, guilt, untold stories, clash of loyalties, and conflict often emerge in families they are working with, and these issues influence not only the functioning of the family but also the work of the professionals who work with them.

It is of paramount importance to address family relationships and dynamics when working with family businesses and families of wealth. Many studies point at the impact of family relationships in processes such as transfer of wealth [legacy transfer] and succession planning.[1] It is well established in the literature that 70% of wealth transitions and business successions fail. It is also recognized that family problems are one of the most common reasons for such failures. This is illustrated by a study by Roy William & Vic Preisser who interviewed 3,200 families that transitioned their wealth. They confirmed that 70% of the families were unsuccessful (failure defined as the "involuntary loss of control of the assets"). The difference between the families that succeeded and those that did not, related not to the wealth-related issues of preservation, taxation, or governance, but to the preparation of heirs to receive and manage wealth. They concluded that "the origins of the 70% failure rate in estate transitions lie *within the family itself.*"[2] Likewise, Morris, M., et.al. reported in their study of 209 family owned businesses that "relationships within the family has the single greatest impact on successful transition."[3]

Issues involving money inevitably stir emotions in families and are often a source of conflict. This is true whether it relates to business succession, estate planning, creation of a foundation, establishing of a family office, or the like.[4,5,6] In his classic book, *Wealth in Families*, Charles Collier[7] wrote that "[m]any factors affect family relationships and money is key among them." He also observed that money has the potential of creating huge problems for family relationships.[7] All family business and wealth advisors touch, in one way or another, on the issue of money in the family.

Human families are complicated systems with multiple layers. Often what seems to be straightforward advice from a professional has less obvious implications in the family. For instance, at first sight it might make sense to recommend that a mother divide her

Introduction

estate in equal parts among her children. In reality, as shown in one of the cases presented here, a decision like this taps hidden complications such as issues about what has been given to whom in the past, which child has helped the mother more and feels deserving of more, how the mother's own experience as a recipient of an inheritance informs her approach to giving, and more. The underlying forces that govern family life often get in the way of solutions proposed by advisors.

This problem is well known in the family enterprise field. In their book, *Advising Family Business*, David Bork, et.al wrote that "Professional advisors who work with family business face a dilemma: the family's actions raise issues and create conflicts that deeply affect the advisor's activity . . . as many as half of the cases are adversely affected by family conflict."[8] Accordingly, solely addressing the legal, financial, or business aspect when advising a family, and ignoring family dynamics, is a serious mistake. Conversely, paying attention to emotions and relationships helps the professional accomplish the technical task at hand.

Bowen family systems theory, applied in the cases presented in this book, provides a theoretical framework for identifying and addressing emotional and relationship issues that need attention. This theory describes the forces that govern relationships and explain the factors that favor better family functioning.[9,10] Throughout each case the authors offer insights about how systems theory explains emotions and family relationships, and how this knowledge informs the advisor's interventions. At the end of each case, there is a more thorough discussion of the theory as it applies to the particular circumstances of that case.

This book is directed to advisors who want to enhance their understanding of family dynamics related to family wealth and family businesses. It provides a basic understanding of the factors underlying family relationships that impact the decision-making process in entrepreneurial families. It discusses which approaches for dealing with family dynamics are more successful, and which lead to common pitfalls.

Four real-life case, with identifying information altered to ensure confidentiality, are presented with detailed analysis of the background, interventions, and outcomes. The cases represent a wide range of outcomes: from a family that mainly accomplished their goals, to families that achieved some success yet were left with remaining problems, to a case that did not result in a successful outcome. These cases represent the spectrum of possibilities in terms of the level of tension and conflict within the family encountered by the authors, which presumably represent the typical variation in any professional practice. Each case yields a series of lessons that can be generalized to similar families. In addition, brief practical takeaways are provided. They constitute interventions that advisors can apply in their work with families. The last chapter presents a discussion of Bowen family systems theory and other relevant knowledge about emotional functioning and family dynamics that provide the theoretical and empirical support of this work.

Professionals are encouraged to address some of the emotional and relationship aspects that arise during their engagement with families, but they are also encouraged to recognize situations that require an expert in behavioral science and to then make appropriate referrals.

Introduction

SOURCES

(1) De Massis, A. (2008) Factors Preventing Intra-Family Succession. *Family Business Review*, Vol, 21 Issue:2, pp183-199.

(2) Williams, R., Preisser, V. (2003) *Preparing Hers. Five Steps to a Successful Transition of Family Wealth and Values.* San Francisco, CA: Robert De Reed Publishers.

(3) Morris, M., Williams, R., Nel, D. (1996) Factors influencing family business succession. *International Journal of Entrepreneurial Behavior & Research*, Vol. 2 Issue: 3, pp.68-81.

(4) Robbins, T. (2014) *Money Master Game. 7 Simple Steps to Financial Freedom.* New York: Simon and Schuster.

(5) Gordon, G., Nicholson, N. (2010) *Family Wars. Stories and Insights from Famous Family Business Feuds.* London, Philadelphia, New Dehli: Kogan Page.

(6) Marcovici, P. (2016) *The Destructive Power of Family Wealth. A guide to succession planning, asset protection, taxation and wealth management.* United Kingdom: John Wiley & Sons.

(7) Collier, Ch. (2008) *Wealth in Families.* Second Edition. Boston, MA: Harvard University.

(8) Bork, D., Jaffe, D. T., Lane S. H., Dashew, L., Heisler, Q.G. (1996) *Working with Family Businesses. A Guide for Professionals.* San Francisco, CA: Jossey-Bass.

(9) Bowen, M. (1978) *Family Therapy in Clinical Practice.* New York, London: Jason Aronson.

(10) Rodriguez, M., Martinez, M. (2014) *La Teoría Familiar Sistémica de Bowen. Avances y Aplicaciones Terapéuticas.* Madrid: McGraw Hill.

CHAPTER 1

OVERLOOKING FAMILY RELATIONSHIPS THAT CREATED AN IMPASSE

The efforts to mediate with the Weinstein family were far from successful. What went wrong? Was there a better way for this professional to handle the problems the family presented? How could a knowledge of Bowen family systems theory have made a difference?

Background

Falcon Group was the brainchild of Nancy Weinstein, a brilliant entrepreneur. Following graduation from college, Nancy started work as a pharmaceutical sales representative. During her visits to physician's offices, Nancy noticed the antiquated manner in which most physicians maintained their records. She used her observations to develop one of the very first electronic medical records software programs (EMR), a program that became a leader in the field long before the widespread adoption of such programs. The code that was written for the program was useful for many purposes, and the program eventually drew great interest. Ultimately, the code was sold to Microsoft for $25M.

With the sales proceeds in hand, Nancy turned to other ventures. She started two other companies. The first was formed to invest in commercial real estate ventures in the Washington, D.C. metro area. The other was formed to invest in securities of both publicly-held companies and technology companies. There were outside investors in both ventures, including cousins of both Nancy and her husband, Robert, but Nancy maintained control of both. The combined ventures were very successful, and their (Falcon Group) value grew to $110M.

The Family

Robert was an engineer by professional training and was in a state of semi-retirement at the time of the professional engagement described here. Robert was withdrawn, even shy, in stark contrast to the gregarious, somewhat aggressive Nancy. They had two adult daughters, Christine and Emily. Christine was President of the investment company. Nancy served as Chairman of the Board of the Falcon Group, and in that sense, Christine ultimately reported to Nancy.

Christine, who graduated with honors from Wharton, was as brilliant as Nancy. She worked for several years at Goldman Sachs before returning to the family business to lead the investment company. She began to feel stifled in the business and felt that

Overlooking Family Relationships That Created an Impasse

she would always be in Nancy's shadow if she did not strike out on her own. Aware of Christine's growing restlessness, and at the insistence of some of the investors in the Falcon Group, Christine signed an executive employment agreement that granted Christine a generous compensation package and a small amount of equity in Falcon Group, but also narrowly defined the circumstances in which her employment could be terminated "for cause." Emily was a senior executive for an aerospace company. She was not involved in the Falcon Group. Her personality was very similar to her father's.

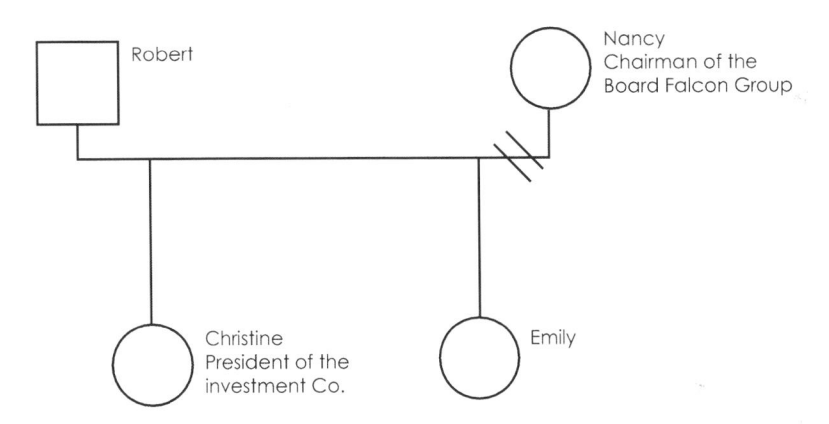

[Genogram: Robert (deceased) —⫽— Nancy, Chairman of the Board Falcon Group; children: Christine, President of the investment Co.; Emily]

For a period, Nancy and Christine coexisted, keeping any tensions between them under wraps. However, once Christine became more vocal to Nancy about wanting a more public role as President of the investment company, tensions began to emerge. Additional tensions emerged as Nancy began estate planning, raising the issue of succession planning for the Falcon Group. First months went by, then two years passed without the implementation of any plan. Christine grew increasingly impatient. Conflict broke out into the open when a trade publication interviewed Christine. She made comments that indicated the most successful investment strategies employed by the investment company were her approaches rather than Nancy's. While the comment contained no direct criticism of Nancy, Nancy took it as a deep personal affront.

In a public manner, Nancy fired Christine from her position as President of the investment company. She alleged that Christine's comments in the interview amounted to insubordination, and thus she could be fired for cause. In doing so, Nancy ignited a family war. Christine responded within days by suing the investment company and the Falcon Group for wrongful termination. She also sued Nancy for breach of her fiduciary obligations related to the Falcon Group. When Robert made it clear to Nancy that he was unhappy with her actions, he returned home one evening to find the locks on the doors of their home changed. He responded shortly thereafter by filing a divorce petition against her. Emily was soon drawn into the war, occasionally as an ally of Nancy, but also allied with her father and sister on some issues, particularly the issue of whether Nancy had managed the Falcon Group in an appropriate manner.

Insight:
Extreme and disproportionate reactions, such as the ones displayed by this family (suing a family member, changing the locks at a home, filing for divorce without previous conversations, etc.), suggest that family tensions had been brewing for decades, maybe even generations. When family members deal with their differences in such a radical way, it is fair to assume that there is a high level of ongoing tension (chronic anxiety) in the group, and it can be predicted that they will take polarized positions and make impulsive, emotionally-driven decisions.

Overlooking Family Relationships That Created an Impasse

The litigation began and proceeded for about a year. The impact on the family was evident. Many embarrassing details the Weinsteins would have preferred to keep private were publicly exposed, such as Nancy's abusiveness to Falcon Group executives. The total cost for the first year of all the litigation was over $2M. At this point, one of the lawyers for Christine suggested that the parties submit their disputes to binding arbitration. While Nancy quickly rejected it, one of her lawyers was subsequently able to persuade her that it made sense to engage in private, non-binding mediation. The proposal was made to Christine, Nancy, and Robert. Robert communicated that he was disinclined to participate in the mediation, but Christine and Nancy agreed.

Insight:
Robert missed an opportunity to attempt to find solutions to a problem he was part of. He did not acknowledge that as husband, father, and investor he was not only a participant in the matter but a key player. His hesitation to become actively involved and explore the contributions he could make, limited the range of possible solutions.

The Engagement

A mediator was engaged for the purpose of seeking resolution of the disputes between Nancy and Christine. The solution would be limited by Robert's stated reluctance to participate.

Nancy

The mediator began by interviewing Nancy. Despite the rules of the mediation explicitly stating that all discussions were to be treated with confidence and the mediator communicating his strong preference to meet with Nancy alone, Nancy insisted on bringing her counsel. There was no practical way to insist that Nancy not bring her lawyer. She frequently consulted with counsel before answering a question.

> **Insight:**
> *Nancy's caution and suspicion suggest a heightened sensitivity to perceived danger and a high level of tension. The mediator had the challenge of remaining focused, managing the emotions in the room, and not allowing the anxiety to derail the engagement, which often happens when people are guarded and stressed.*

Nancy's point of view was that she was the dominant force behind all of Falcon's success, and that Christine had made very few original contributions, certainly none of any great worth. Similarly, she expressed that as her mother, she had given Christine all of the educational, travel and other opportunities a child could have or want. She referred to Christine as an "ingrate" who did not credit Nancy for Christine's financial and business success.

Nancy also complained at some length about the investors in Falcon, particularly Robert's cousins, who often pressed her at shareholder meetings regarding the details of investments and the compensation she received, and had also complained at a recent meeting about the firing of Christine. Even though it was beyond the scope of any issue the mediator wanted to explore, Nancy volunteered her view of Robert, who in her opinion was a selfish, ungrateful man, who never showed adequate appreciation for all that Nancy had done for him.

Overlooking Family Relationships That Created an Impasse

When pressed at the end of the meeting to express what her goals were, Nancy had a very hard time articulating them, beyond saying that she wanted to see Christine "defeated and humiliated."

Insight:

When an individual perceives him/herself cornered, it is hard to have the perspective required to develop constructive goals. Instead, energy is directed towards others, often to attack them and to defend from them. Better outcomes are associated when people have clear, realistic, and positive goals. One of the tasks of a professional consultant is to help the client develop such goals.

Christine

Christine met separately (and alone) with the mediator a few days after Nancy and her counsel had met with him. While Christine was more measured in tone than Nancy was, she also expressed a great deal of resentment. As an adult, she indicated that she felt none of her achievements were adequately acknowledged or rewarded by Nancy. Nancy did not attend any of her graduations, yet routinely referred to Christine as "the daughter who graduated with honors at Wharton." At no point in the conversation did Christine give any sense that she believed she had contributed to the mother-daughter dynamic that developed over the years.

While Christine credited her mother with having "great entrepreneurial instincts," she persuasively explained that in fact the investment strategies she used grew out of a thesis she composed at Wharton and were refined during her time working at Goldman Sachs. In fact, Christine went so far as to bring a copy of that thesis to the meeting and to refer to specific passages of it during the mediator meeting. Despite crediting her mother's instincts, Christine was also quick to state that her mother did not understand the public capital markets, and in fact, repeated comments made to her by securities analysts that Nancy's contributions during analyst conference calls were "bizarre and irrelevant."

In conclusion, Christine indicated that she wanted a fair resolution of the disputes but strongly preferred not to be in business with Nancy any longer.

> **Insight:**
>
> *Such an intense parent-child relationship as the one described by Nancy and Christine precludes both parent and child from sustaining a sense of individuality, that is, an identity separate from each other. Nancy's description of her daughter's success as the result of her own efforts and Christine's fierce independence from mother speaks about the degree of fusion between them. A parent's view of a child as part of herself is reciprocated by a child whose life energy is oriented either towards or away from the parent. This represents a very challenging configuration for the professional because such relationships often resort to cutoff in an attempt to deal with the anxiety emerging from the fusion.*

The Professional's Evaluation and Interventions

After considering what he had learned in the meetings with Nancy and Christine, the mediator believed that there was some possibility of resolution. While there was significant disagreement

Overlooking Family Relationships That Created an Impasse

and deep animosity between them, Nancy and Christine both expressed concern about the financial impact of the litigation. Also, both agreed that they needed to go their separate ways. Moreover, the mediator learned that the investors in the Falcon Group (many of whom were, as noted above, extended family members) had exerted great pressure on Nancy to restore Christine, as they credited her with the success of the investment company, and thus the driver of the success of their investment in Falcon Group.

The most obvious solution would in substance be to cause the "split up" of Falcon Group, with the investment company and real estate company being divided into two separate stand-alone companies. The idea would be to either redeem or significantly reduce Nancy's interest in the investment company, in favor of an increase of her interest in the real estate company. This would allow Christine to return as President of the investment company. Christine, who by this point had become a consultant for a venture fund that invested in emerging market equities, indicated she would be willing to return to the investment company. The arrangement would not disturb any outside investor's holdings in the sense that they would exchange their interest in Falcon Group for direct interests in both the investment company and the real estate investment company. Based on the feedback from both Christine and Nancy, as well as the intelligence the mediator gathered regarding the outside investors, he believed that this plan would be acceptable in concept. It was also possible that even a significant reduction of Nancy's interest in the investment company might not be enough, as Christine expressed reluctance to return if Nancy was even a minority shareholder in the investment company.

The mediator believed that because the value of Nancy's interest in the investment company was so significant, the arrangement would only work if Robert became involved. As noted above, Robert was very hesitant to become involved in the mediation. When the mediator did contact him, however, Robert clearly stated that he would be willing to become engaged if it benefited Christine, but otherwise, he had no desire to participate in mediation or to maintain any interest in Falcon Group. Inasmuch as the interest Nancy held in Falcon Group was marital property in the jurisdiction where Robert and Nancy resided during their marriage, the mediator saw an opportunity to resolve some of the differences between Robert and Nancy as well. The idea in essence would be for Robert to trade the indirect interest he would have in the real estate venture in exchange for a larger interest in the investment company.

Insight:
Any mother-child relationship evolves in the context of the relationship with father. In this way, the parental triangle (or primary triangle) is formed by father, mother, and child. This triangle stays active, and is powerful and emotionally-charged, even when the child is an adult. A parental triangle can have different qualities at different points in time. In this case the triangle seemed to be characterized by Robert and Christine agreeing (the "insiders") and opposing mother. Nancy resented the "outsider" position, which is usually the most uncomfortable position in a relationship triangle, and predictably reacted with upset.

The difficult issue therefore became the valuation of the interest Nancy held in the investment company through her ownership in Falcon Group. There seemed to be general agreement that the value of the interest the Weinstein's held in Falcon Group approximated $45M. After some initial discussions with all sides and their respective advisors, it became apparent that there was in fact contention over the issue of respective valuations of the investment company and the real estate investment company. On the one hand, Robert and Christine believed that the investment company was worth approximately 50% more than the real estate investment company. On the other hand, Nancy took the position that the value of the investment company was worth almost twice that of the real estate investment company. Neither party was necessarily right or wrong: there was difficulty in establishing true value of some of the real estate company's properties, as well as the securities held by the investment company in private (non-public companies). The bottom-line reality was that the no matter whose valuation was used, it would not have been possible to completely "cash out" Nancy from the investment company with a simple swap of interests.

Insight:
The difficulty in establishing definite facts around the valuation of each of the companies contributed to a discussion based more on perceptions and subjectivity than on verifiable facts. This in itself made the discussion more heated and emotional, thus more difficult to manage.

The discussions and negotiations around valuation opened some old wounds for Christine, who interpreted what she regarded as Nancy's inflated valuation of the investment company as an attempt by Nancy to maintain a significant interest in the investment company, and therefore control over Christine. Christine grew increasingly uncomfortable with the prospect of Nancy remaining even as a minority stockholder in the investment company. In response, the mediator hypothetically inquired whether it might be possible for the investment company to purchase back from Nancy whatever shares were not exchanged with Robert as part of the mediator's proposal. The answer was that it was possible, although some of the securities it held would have to be sold to generate the required cash.

After multiple proposals and counterproposals, the parties were approximately $3M apart in their valuation of Nancy's interest in the investment company. Informal evaluations indicated that the value of Robert and Nancy's marital estate was close to $100M, so a difference of $3M – which at most meant that, even using Nancy's numbers, the parties were only approximately $1.5M apart in the value of the interest that Nancy would retain in the investment company post-divorce – was not in the overall analysis a significant financial issue. Discussions then temporarily stalled.

Insight:

A practical solution was available. It became clearer and clearer that the problem was not a lack of a logical and fair monetary arrangement, but rather that the problem had a significant emotional aspect hindering a resolution of the conflict. Nevertheless, none of that was addressed and the mediator continued to push for the completion of a plan that, appropriate in itself, was unlikely to succeed. This often happens when there is no attention paid to the emotional and relationship elements of a business decision.

Overlooking Family Relationships That Created an Impasse

The mediator proposed to both sides that they and their advisers gather in his office in separate rooms, so that the mediator could efficiently work with both in an attempt to bridge the differences. The mediator reminded both of them of the relatively small difference in value. He cajoled, argued, persuaded, even used the prospect of doom of what would be the outcomes if they did not reach agreement.

Nancy strenuously objected to the mediator's interventions and cursed at him at one point but offered to reduce her valuation of her interest in the investment company interest to a sum that was only $2M higher than Robert and Christine's valuation. At that point, the mediator walked down the hall of his office to communicate Nancy's concession to Christine (who also was speaking for Robert on this issue), and to see whether she could offer any movement in response. Far from it: Christine insisted that she could do no more, and that she felt she had "already given too much." Christine often complained about Nancy's inflexibility, but at this point it was Nancy who offered movement while Christine refused.

The mediator walked back down the hall and informed Nancy of Christine's position. Nancy exploded, saying that she would not offer anything further, and screaming so loud that after the meeting, one of Christine's lawyers said she could hear Nancy screaming from down the hall. Nancy then stormed out.

Both parties withdrew from mediation at that point.

Insight:
This episode represents a typical situation in a conflictual relationship where the "timing" seems to always be off: when

one party becomes reasonable, the other becomes unreasonable; when one wants to talk, the other refuses; when one is flexible, the other is rigid, all this happening in a coordinated and complementary fashion. This pattern is destined to continue and any solution to be elusive unless someone sees the dynamic and does something about it.

The Aftermath

Upon the failure of mediation, the litigation dragged on for years, further harming the wealth of the Weinstein family. Little progress was made in stabilizing the finances of Falcon Group, which declined as a result of the litigation and related issues. A coterie of professional advisors came and went, but none addressed the relationship problems and the emotional aspects involved. One senior family business advisor remarked at one session that the parties seemed to be intent on war, that only war could bring about a result that they would accept, even though that result might be worse than the one they could have achieved through negotiation. The only factor that finally stopped the bleeding was that despite the family's wealth, it experienced a cash drain and selling their respective interests in Falcon Group at a distressed price became the only realistic option. They did so, and the verdicts in the various litigation matters produced neither a clear winner nor a clear loser.

Christine raised funds to start a hedge fund and became its manager, creating a successful career. The relationship between Nancy and Christine was irretrievably broken. Two years after the litigation, Nancy developed cancer and died within a year. There was no reconciliation between them before Nancy's death.

Commentary on the Emotional Aspect of the Process

The failure to find a resolution in the case of Falcon Group is unfortunate but common example of one in which wealth and family relationships are damaged. In the aftermath of the consultation, the mediator reflected on the factors that made this case unsuccessful, as well as on the unexplored alternatives that might have changed the outcome. These alternatives can be summarized in the following areas: a) Overlooking the emotional process and family dynamics involved in the interaction and over-focusing on the financial and legal solutions. (*Overlooking emotions and family dynamics*), b) The mediator's failure to define appropriate boundaries between himself and the clients (*Blurred boundaries*), c) Missing the opportunity to establish bridges with other professionals involved in the engagement *(Lack of connection with other professionals)*, and d) Failing to engage other resources within the family *(Untapped resources within the family)*.

Overlooking emotions and family dynamics

Most human problems are multilayered. Family businesses problems are no exception. The financial and legal aspects of the business are important to address, but equally so is the aspect relating to emotions and family dynamics. The mediator in the Falcon Group case was aware of the intensity of emotions and of the family problems but focused only on crafting a financial and legal solution without addressing the relationship obstacles. He worked hard to create a reasonable solution, one which was appropriate in theory, without accounting for the strength of the emotional factors that eventually defeated the plan. He underestimated the power of the family dynamics involved.

It is impossible to know what would have happened if family relationships were directly addressed, but this case invites some speculation. What might have happened if improving family relationships were part of the process? Conversations with each family member about how this problem came to be might have prepared the way for a practical solution. There is a chance that if each individual slightly changed the perception of their own position, felt less cornered and threatened, and assumed more responsibility for their part in the problem, the outcome would have been better.

It might have been worth taking the time to explore the family history, the creation of the family business, the good and the difficult times, the sacrifices, and the challenges in creating such a successful family business, along with related topics. Perhaps helping the Weinstein's to see themselves as a family in a different light would have shifted, even if so slightly, the perception they had about self and each other. In other words, not addressing the emotional aspect of the problem was the "elephant in the room." Failing to address the family dynamics was an omission that likely obstructed efforts to find solutions at other levels.

Blurred boundaries

Defining boundaries between self and other (in this case between the mediator and the clients) requires the capacity to represent one's own ethical standards and the ability to be clear about what one will and will not do. It also means the ability to know where one's responsibilities end, and others' responsibilities begin.

A common mistake made by professionals, which is a result of a poor definition of such boundaries, is the over-investment in a particular outcome. When this happens, the client – who should be the party most committed to solving the problem – loses hold of the situation and fails to do what is needed to attain the goal. In this case the mediator knew that the resolution was difficult. He invested himself more and more in finding an agreement. As he did so, the clients became less and less willing to do what it took to attain resolution. It is possible that this approach (being overly invested), hindered the capacity of Nancy and Christine to be flexible and willing to compromise.

Another example of the mediator not establishing appropriate boundaries was when he asked Nancy about her goals for the engagement and she responded that she wanted Christine "defeated and humiliated." The mediator, despite the fact that he did not see this as a worthwhile goal, neither challenged nor discussed Nancy's response. A more direct and in-depth conversation about this issue could have better aligned the efforts of the mediator with those of his client. Such clarity and alignment of goals give the consultation direction and a higher probability of reaching a desired outcome.

To establish clear and appropriate boundaries between the family and the professional, the professional must speak freely and confidently about his/her view of the problem. Often, this is not an easy task for the professional because that view is different from what the client would like to hear. Nevertheless, when the professional is firm in their position and is able to communicate it in a clear and respectful manner, the client benefits.

Lack of connection with other professionals

The situation with the Weinstein family was very tense. Given the inflexible positions the family members acquired, the mediator was left little room to maneuver. When this is the case, an alternative is to create a wider, less rigid web of connections, often attained by establishing direct contact with professionals who are representing the different parties involved. Christine and Nancy each had a lawyer, so did Robert (a divorce lawyer). The mediator did not attempt to reach out to them. With these professionals he might have been able to discuss matters more directly and productively, and in turn, the respective clients perhaps could have heard messages with more openness. When relationship triangles are too rigid, such as in this case of Nancy, Christine, and Robert, activating other interlocking triangles has the potential to loosen tensions.

Untapped resources within the family

It is an indication of strength in a family to be able to reach for outside help. Paradoxically, one of the roles of a family advisor is to help the family recognize their own capabilities and activate their own resources.

The Weinstein family was at a point where they could not reach an agreement regarding their differences. In the face of stagnation, the mediator did not consider looking for other family members who could have been a resource in such difficult moments. Perhaps, other family members would have been helpful in identifying avenues for resolution.

The mediator limited his field of vision to Nancy and Christine. He might have benefitted from getting the perspective of other family members, starting with Richard and Emily, who possibly had some influence with Christine and Nancy, respectively. The

Overlooking Family Relationships That Created an Impasse

only effort the mediator made to contact Richard was an invitation to the mediation table, which he refused. There could have been other ways to engage him in the process.

In addition, the mediator could have communicated with the extended family involved in the business. Listening to the views of others might have helped him better understand the difficult position both Nancy and Christine were in. Contact with cousins would have surely provided information that would have expanded the alternatives going forward.

When families are stuck, useful questions to ask are: "Who in this family has the ability to be in open contact with others?" "Who could maintain the most objective perspective?" "Who can be most neutral and least emotional about the issue?" These questions identify potential family leaders who can help the group move in a better direction. Exploring a family's resources and encouraging a family to build greater internal capabilities requires more work, but usually yields better results.

Final Comments

The results of these events were very serious for the Weinstein family. After many millions spent in litigation, the family was no further ahead than when the difficulties started. It is likely the stress contributed to Nancy's deteriorating health and ultimately to her death. The family was left depleted in many ways.

The discussion about what might have been is a speculative exercise, of course. There is no way to know whether things would have been different. Nevertheless, mistakes invite reflection. The

Falcon Group case illustrates the potential benefit of approaching complex problems with a wider perspective. A system view has the potential to account for the emotions and family dynamics, which in conjunction with the financial, legal, and organizational elements, provide a comprehensive understanding of the family business' challenges. The Falcon Investment/Weinstein case invites us to think about what was missed in the original analysis. It invites professionals to see *the blind spots.*

Lessons Learned

This case produced important lessons that can be applied to other cases. First, the impact of emotional process and family dynamics has the power to support or damage any solution to a business or financial problem the family faces. Failing to account for the impact of the emotional process may make the difference between a workable solution and a disaster.

Second, the professional has the responsibility of communicating to the family his best assessment of a problem, including his/her estimation of the part that relationships play. If the advisor is not equipped to deal with the emotional aspect of the problem, the advisor can recommend the inclusion of a relationship expert on the working team. The family might or might not accept the proposal, but the recommendation opens new alternatives.

Lastly, families often have resources which are not exploited. When that possibility is considered, family members, non-family members, and other professionals may emerge as previously unidentified assets to be utilized to broaden the view. Engaging

Overlooking Family Relationships That Created an Impasse

with more individuals in the group can be instrumental for the implementation of a solution and plan.

Key Takeaways

- Take into consideration the emotional process and family dynamics in a family business. Do not underestimate the power of emotions and relationships.

- If emotions are getting in the way of a solution, address the issue openly. Invite a relationship specialist to join the team if needed.

- Create new relationship triangles that can help dissolve tensions. Connect with other professionals with a spirit of collaboration in favor of the family.

- Be clear about your own understanding of the problem and communicate it clearly to the family. Be honest and direct when describing your thinking.

- Connect with family members not currently involved in the situation. Seek other members who have the ability to relate to most individuals in the group, have an objective understanding of the problem, and are capable of being neutral.

CHAPTER 2

AN ASSET DISTRIBUTION PLAN THAT PRODUCED FAMILY ACRIMONY

A mother was finalizing her estate plan and in connection with that, provided an asset distribution plan to her three sons that was designed to reflect an equal allocation of assets. To her surprise, the disclosure ignited a firestorm of controversy among the three sons that threatened to not only frustrate the mother's goals but also to embroil the family in litigation.

Background

Charles Wilson, a lover of fine art, antiques, and other valuable collectibles, turned his avocation into a business shortly before the onset of World War II. He started a business that purchased, held, and sold such merchandise. The business grew steadily over time,

Seeing the Blind Spot

enough to sustain a lavish lifestyle enjoyed by him, his wife, and their only daughter, Virginia (born in 1934).

The Family

Charles died in 1962, shortly after which the business was taken over by Virginia's husband, Jerome. Virginia was only too happy to have Jerome take over. She enjoyed the beauty and value of the works her father collected, but she did not have the desire to attend auctions, cultivate the relationships that provided access to private collections, or attend to other administrative activities regarding the business. Jerome and Virginia had one child, Anthony, who was born in 1959. Jerome competently managed the business for a few years before unexpectedly dying in 1966 when Anthony was six years old.

Within a year of being widowed, Virginia married Richard, equally skilled at managing the business. She had two sons with

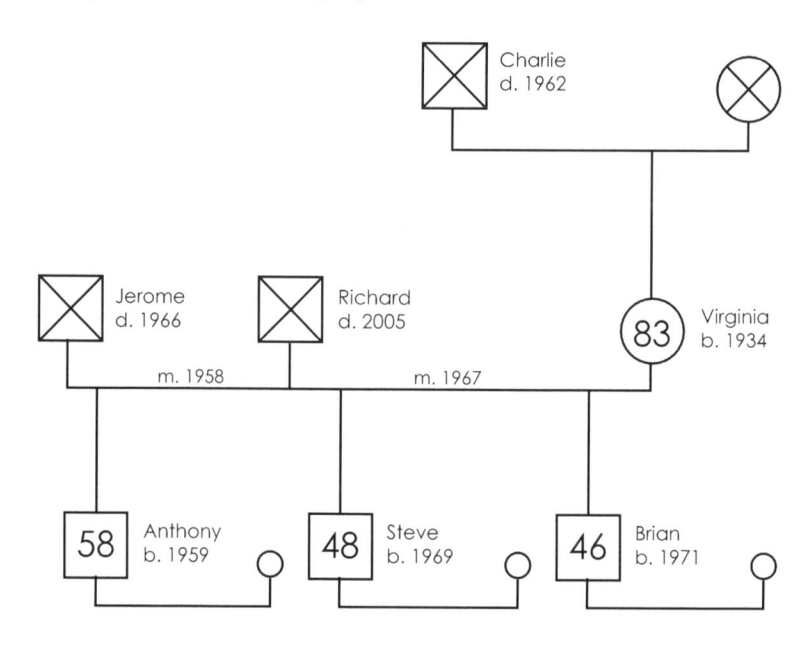

An Asset Distribution Plan that Produced Family Acrimony

Richard, Steven and Brian, who were born in 1969 and 1971, respectively. Many years passed, and the business continued to operate profitably, but without growth in any measurable sense. In the interim, Anthony was elected state senator, Steven started an engineering services company, and Brian became a high school teacher. Richard passed away in 2005.

After Richard passed away, the business was run for a few years by a skilled and trusted employee. Shortly after her 80th birthday, Virginia concluded that it was time to finalize her estate plan. Once none of the sons expressed any interest in taking over the business, and in the absence of a likely acquirer, she concluded it was time to liquidate and dissolve the business. Her intention was to divide her estate among her three sons equally, which in addition to her other assets, included the assets of the business. She informed her three sons of that plan and went so far as to create a draft asset distribution plan that related to personal property. She circulated this to her three sons. It immediately produced intense acrimony. First, Brian believed that he had been promised certain assets that in the asset distribution plan were designated for another son. And second, Anthony and Brian interpreted the plan as misleading, because it omitted any description of real property and intangibles that they believed were very valuable.

The family tensions that were ignited by the draft asset distribution plans had been emerging for some time. At one earlier point, Brian had confronted his mother about an issue and it became contentious. Virginia fainted, sustained a concussion, and had to be rushed to the emergency room. As events unfolded, it became clear that those angry confrontations had been a regular occurrence, mostly between Brian and Virginia, but also between Anthony and Virginia, and sometimes including their spouses. Beyond that, Virginia believed that a few months prior to this episode, Brian had taken some of the paintings that were the property of the business. She was infuriated, seeing no other solution but to sue her son. Her relationship with Steven had been more peaceful.

Virginia's health had been deteriorating for some time, and the stress of the family conflicts accelerated the decline. Her doctors recommended that Virginia avoid family quarrels because such stress was very detrimental to her health.

Insight:

These events reveal a long-standing turmoil and high levels of anxiety in Virginia's family. This was expressed by intense conflict and extreme behaviors such as confrontations between mother and sons, Brian taking valuables without the necessary conversations with his mother, and Virginia fainting during a contentious conversation. Anxiety in systems spreads infectiously and events such as the ones described, amplify the tensions. Relationships fueled by anxiety have the potential of escalating into severe conflict and/or dysfunction in one or more of the individuals.

The Engagement

Virginia was referred to a law firm by her financial advisor, who was concerned that the severe tensions between the family members could lead to litigation, specifically between Virginia and Brian over the disputed paintings. Both the lawyer and the financial

An Asset Distribution Plan that Produced Family Acrimony

advisor concluded that engaging in legal battle would represent an enormous source of stress for Virginia. In their judgment, it would also jeopardize her health, her financial position, and of course, her long-term relationship with her sons. Nevertheless, it was only prudent that she be prepared, and so arrangements were made to have a litigator ready if needed.

Insight:

Anxiety is the response to a real or imagined threat. One of the natural responses of an organism that perceives threat is to attack. As anxiety increases, so does the likelihood of interpretation of cues as threatening and dangerous. Consequently, more attacking behavior is produced. In this case, it is likely that Virginia came to interpret her sons' behaviors as threatening and that those behaviors activated her fight response. Likewise, Anthony and Brian perceived being wronged and attacked their mother in return. It was important to deactivate these responses in order to achieve Virginia's goals.

Virginia's goals

The lawyer proceeded to have extensive conversations with Virginia which explored her family history, the sources of family tensions, and her estate planning goals. During those first conversations, she had no persuasive explanation for what had angered two of her sons so deeply. She communicated that she wanted to benefit her three sons to the same degree. The proposed equal division of her estate amongst her sons sounded reasonable and common, so it was unlikely that the asset distribution plan alone could be the source of the animosity. When pressed, Virginia vaguely responded that Anthony and Brian seemed upset with what they perceived as her favoritism toward Steven.

In relation to the decision-making surrounding her estate, Virginia insisted that she wanted to do things her own way, regardless of her son's opinions, stating "it's my money." As conversations progressed, however, she also expressed her desire to achieve some level of peace with Anthony and Brian before she died, which might require modifications to her estate plan. Virginia finally acknowledged that those desires were potentially in conflict. She became more open to the option of making some undefined adjustments to her estate plan as a gesture to achieve some peace.

Insight:

A very important function of a professional is to help clients clarify their goals. This takes time and sometimes lengthy conversations. Often this analysis reveals that the goals the client expresses are conflicting, therefore work has to be done to make them consistent before proceeding with any action. It is predictable that without resolving this discrepancy, Virginia would have found any result from the professional engagement unsatisfactory.

The Professional's Evaluation and Interventions

The lawyer knew that if he wanted to assemble a fuller picture of the situation before providing additional advice to Virginia, he needed to obtain further information. With this in mind, he contacted all other family members.

An Asset Distribution Plan that Produced Family Acrimony

The three sons and their spouses were individually consulted by phone multiple times. Initially, their demeanor was suspicious and guarded, often commenting that they saw the lawyer as nothing more than a "hired gun" to do Virginia's bidding. The lawyer kept in mind the importance of approaching each family member in an open manner, and as the history of the family was revealed, it became clear that the relationships among several members of the family had been troubled from an early stage.

From the perspectives of all three sons, Virginia's second husband, Richard, was a tyrant. He was abusive towards the children and their mother. After Steven went away for schooling when he was a teenager, it appeared that Brian became the principal object of Richard's angry explosions. There was a sense amongst the children that Virginia had turned a blind eye toward Richard's behavior. Virginia also revealed to her attorney, that she had been fostering competition among her sons since an early age with the idea that it would make them "tougher".

From the standpoint of Anthony and Brian, Steven was always favored by Virginia. Both believed that Virginia made efforts to protect and benefit Steven through the years that she did not extend to either of them. Steven's perspective was not to dispute any of the positions of his brothers. In fact, he sought to avoid any discussion of the issues they raised, but rather focused on his mother's health and well-being. Further, Steven acknowledged that he was away from the family home during some of the worst times, and so did not witness any abuse Richard directed in that period, to Brian in particular.

Insight:

A family's style of relating is established in its early stages of development. Such style becomes somewhat fixed and it is easily activated in future situations. For Virginia's family, fierce attacking and defending had become part of their relationship repertoire and not surprisingly this was the "first line of response" as they engaged in conversations about the estate distribution plan. Over the years, all of them had become exquisitely sensitive to each other's attention, approval, support, expectations, and upsets. Such sensitivities made it hard to talk without quick reaction. A professional has to be aware that it requires great effort for family members to bypass these automatic reactions in order to reach a calmer, more thoughtful approach.

The focus for Anthony's and Brian's current acrimony seemed to be an investment that Virginia and Richard had made in Steven's engineering services business. Both Anthony and Brian were unhappy that the details of that investment were not contemporaneously disclosed to them. They also believed that the investment represented a very large portion of Virginia's estate in which they thought they would have no share. This somewhat explained Anthony and Brian's disagreement and upset in relation to the proposed distribution of their mother's estate. In addition, Brian was particularly attached to certain art objects that had sentimental value for him, and he was convinced that his mother and he had come to a previous agreement that made him the owner of those items. He was appalled by his mother's accusations that he had stolen these items.

Knowing the brothers perceived themselves as being disadvantaged, the lawyer communicated to Virginia the need that she be

An Asset Distribution Plan that Produced Family Acrimony

transparent if there was any hope of achieving her goal of peace with Anthony and Brian.

Insight:

Sibling rivalry is a common occurrence in families, but in this case, it was extreme. The history of the family alerted the lawyer about the extent to which these siblings were susceptible to feeling disadvantaged. It gave him a measure of the work needed to satisfy a sense of fairness.

In order to try to advance her interests, the lawyer recommended that Virginia provide the details of the investment in Steven's company to Anthony and Brian. Virginia agreed, and so an accounting was prepared relating to that investment which included canceled checks, records of the partial repayments made by Steven, records of the distributions made by the engineering services company and so on. While this information did not provide immediate calm, the records showed that the magnitude of the investment was far smaller than Anthony and Brian believed. Virginia also explained in writing that in fact, her estate plan provided that the investment in Steven's engineering services company would be divided equally among the three sons, which alone reduced some tension.

Slowly, the conversations became more objective, and less emotional and hostile. There were several family phone calls to discuss all the matters Virginia had disclosed, which focused on the details of the investment rather than on intimate family matters. These phone calls were productive in clarifying the facts and in communicating Virginia's intentions.

The Aftermath

After a few months of phone and email communications, Virginia and her sons felt comfortable enough to meet in one place without any professionals, to talk face-to-face about Virginia's health and estate plan. The meeting was difficult but there were no blowups. Shortly thereafter, Virginia traveled to Arizona to spend two weeks with Anthony and his family. The visit got tense a few times, but never to the point where there was any suspension of communications.

Virginia made some modifications to the distribution plan to address the issues raised by Anthony and Brian. For example, she agreed to give Brian certain objects. At the very least these adjustments sent the message to them that she did hear their concerns. The threat of any litigation over the paintings abated.

The consultation with the lawyer ended here. It was evident that the disclosures Virginia made did not remove the sense of favoritism for Steven that Anthony and Brian held. It is uncertain whether the family will be inclined to build on the progress made with this engagement and whether they will ever address the deeper sources of conflict among them.

Commentary on the Emotional Aspect of the Process

This family's experience illustrates these important elements that relate to the emotional aspect of the professional engagement process: a) Current problems have their roots in early family life, (*The importance of family history*), b) The professional is also subject to the emotional undercurrents of the engagement (*The position of the professional and his emotional reactions*), c) Emotionality can be an obstacle to clear thinking (*The process of reaching a more thoughtful position to make better decisions*), and d) The assessment of the level of reactivity in the family helps define the professional's approach to family meetings (*Regulating the intensity of the contact between family members*).

Importance of family history

Exploring the family history gave context to the apparent irrational reactions of Anthony and Brian to Virginia's decisions about her estate. By learning about early events in the family, the lawyer was able to understand the roots of such reactions. Of particular relevance is the fact that this family lost a parent in an untimely manner. Such an event usually represents a significant shock to a family unit, creating great anxiety that is not easily dissolved. The lawyer knew he was dealing with a family with long-standing high levels of anxiety (also referred to as chronic anxiety), which rendered them vulnerable to quick, impulsive, and instinctual reactions.

After Jerome's death, Virginia had found herself widowed with a small child, no parents or siblings, and with a business she had no desire to manage. Virginia and Anthony, who grew up as an only child until the age of 10, probably developed a very tight bond that, on the one hand provided a sense of closeness, and on the other the potential for friction. This relationship pattern was present decades later.

Virginia's quick second marriage and Richard's role in leading the business suggests the creation of a network of dependencies within the family. When these dependencies are too intense, families often become uncomfortable and resort to fighting and violence to deal with them. From the historic vantage point, the contentious and even aggressive behavior between family members represented relationship patterns that were established early on in the life of the family and were deeply rooted. A major challenge for everyone was to override those automatic behaviors and substitute them with more flexible, creative, and adaptive ones.

Another important element revealed by the exploration of the family history was that it was constituted as a blended family. Children in blended families often develop a sense of first and second-class status among them, and there is increased competition for resources such as money, attention, love, and time. Anthony was the only recipient of family resources for an extended period of time, until Steven was born when he was 10 years old. Steven, as the first biological son of the new marriage, had a special place in the family and was very important to both Richard and Virginia. Brian, being the youngest of three boys, was in a position of easily feeling disfavored and disadvantaged, while also feeling entitled to special treatment for being "the youngest." Based on these elements, it is easy to see how Anthony and Brian saw themselves as disadvantaged and how they developed a sensitivity to being treated unfairly and to being "left out." Steven seemed to be in the more comfortable position as the "insider" and as "mother's guardian."

The family history also pointed at strengths in this group. First, despite the problems, they all had a desire to maintain their family ties. Second, family members were able to develop life projects for themselves and follow their own interests. The professional choices of each son represent a capacity to use life energy in a constructive and creative way. This provides a measure of some level of independence and tolerance for differences in the group, which in turn speaks about flexibility. The desire to maintain family ties and some degree of flexibility was instrumental to finding a solution that was agreeable to everybody.

The position of the professional and his emotional reactions

A key factor that made it possible for this family to move forward was the capacity of the lawyer to be fully involved with the family while maintaining a neutral position. This would have been impossible without direct contact with each family member, which allowed him to learn how each family member viewed the history of the problem, and to hear their perspectives and perceptions. It was crucial for him to develop a complete understanding of the problem and to realize that everybody was reacting to what they perceived as unfair treatment and even threat to their well-being. This awareness helped him stay impartial and understand the different points of view.

It is not an easy task for a professional to maintain a detached perspective in such an engagement. In fact, losing that detached perspective is one of the typical landmines when working with families because the professional is also subject to its emotional undercurrents. It might take the form of taking sides, getting angry, feeling sorry for someone, being compelled to fix the problem, distancing from some members, or offering special treatment to others. In this case, the lawyer had to be vigilant because he tended to feel protective of Brian whom he perceived as the most affected and hurt of the family members. Professionals need to always be vigilant about their own reactions when working with families and ensure that his or her responses are not controlled by his own attitudes or emotional history.

More often than not, themes that emerge in the client family tap a sensitive fiber in the consultant, and in that way he/she may bring his/her own personal history and vulnerabilities into the process. In this case, Virginia's revelation that for years she had been promoting active competition between the three brothers as a way of teaching them "to be tough," caused an immediate emotional response in the lawyer. As the lawyer reflected upon his reactions, he saw that he often felt the instinct to criticize Virginia's parenting and to lecture her about better ways of supporting the siblings' relationships. He had to be attentive to his own reactions, identify them, and avoid letting them interfere with his professional services.

In any given interaction, anyone's emotionality can be triggered. A professional that is aware of the emotional dynamic that is taking place both within him/herself and in the interaction with the family, can take a step back, regain a position of an interested observer, and reposition him/herself in an objective and neutral stance, all of which are necessary for effective interventions.

The process of reaching a more thoughtful position to make better decisions

A professional provides a family with information and technical resources to find solutions to a problem. But this is not enough. Clients need to be capable of thinking as clearly as possible for themselves in order to use this information to make better

An Asset Distribution Plan that Produced Family Acrimony

decisions. Reaching a more thoughtful position is difficult when the anxiety in a system is high. Being able to relax allows people to access their higher functions with more ease, and thus allows them to make more dispassionate evaluations of reality and consequently, better decisions. Virginia's family was in a state of such agitation that their capacity to make thoughtful decisions was hampered.

Since the onset of the engagement, the lawyer's clarity and equanimity represented a non-reactive presence that contributed to the decrease of anxiety. Likewise, being in contact with each and all family members and his capacity to effectively communicate to them that he had the whole family's best interest in mind, was important to reduce the tension. A professional can always make a substantial contribution by simply remaining calm and engaged, which alone promotes calming among family members.

Another intervention that helped dissipate the anxiety was the pursuit of factual information. The exploration about the family history, the business, Virginia's estate, and the plans for distribution not only provided the lawyer with important information, but also helped each member reach a calmer state as they described and learned about these facts. Factual questions such as "who," "what," "when," and "how" were more useful than the question "why," which taps on subjectivity and interpretation. Professionals can strive to seek answers to questions which do not invite subjectivity and interpretation. Doing that alone prompts family members to focus on questions that are more productive.

A turning point in bringing all family members to a place where they felt less threatened and anxious was the provision of the accounting relating to Virginia's participation in Steven's business. The effect was not immediate, but the information provided certainly helped to focus more on reality than on perception. Again, verifiable information has the effect of bringing people to a solving process mode that is more grounded on reality and less on perception and interpretation. When there is opportunity for a professional to achieve that in an engagement, the professional should always seek to do so.

Finally, the exploration of the multigenerational family history had a calming effect for the whole system. Some members were able to appreciate that they all dealt with different challenges. This awareness helped them be more understanding of each other's position. Frequently, the description of family developments over multiple generations brings to the foreground the power of the dynamic that all members equally face. Often, family members develop a better appreciation of the underlying tension, or chronic anxiety, that impacts all of them in the present. This appreciation usually opens the door to less guarded positions and more willingness to collaborate.

For this family, describing their past and how they got to the present moment served to attain a more favorable attitude and greater willingness to find a solution agreeable to all. For example, Virginia understood the importance Brian placed on certain objects and thus was willing to make modification to the asset distribution plan. In a way, exploring the family history offered a broader perspective which helped all family members think more clearly.

An Asset Distribution Plan that Produced Family Acrimony

Regulating the intensity of the contact

Although it is desirable for family members to talk directly with each other about their problems, in this case such exchange required some preparatory work. Based on the family history, the lawyer knew that relationships were volatile. It was likely that a premature family session would have resulted in unproductive arguing with mutual accusations, if not overt fighting. Instead, the lawyer laid the ground for future family meetings through individual conversations with each family member and through the clarification of facts.

As the lawyer worked with Virginia to learn about the details of her estate, he maintained communication with the sons and daughters-in-law. At this point the lawyer functioned as a bridge between mother and her sons who were highly reactive to each other, but he kept in mind the importance of eventually promoting direct contact between them.

This is an example in which relationship triangles can be used in a productive fashion. The lawyer served as a link between Virginia and Anthony, and between Virginia and Brian, who had been having difficulties relating directly with each other. The lawyer was cautious to stay in contact with all of them. He also encouraged direct conversation among them, first through writing and then by phone. He communicated that he had the whole family's best interest as a high priority because that was what Virginia had defined as an important interest. He also stated his determination to take reasonable steps to serve these interests.

Eventually, all parties came to a less reactive stance and were able to meet and have a reasonable exchange. Greater transparency about Virginia's goals and intentions, among other factors, brought about the potential for better communication and more work to improve the relationship with one another. For the time being, the family avoided the worst of the outcomes that were (and to some degree, remain) possible.

Final Comments

It is impossible to know what would have happened had the professional engagement taken a different direction. What is unquestionable is that the efforts of the family and the intervention of the lawyer had positive results. After all, for the time being, the wealth was preserved rather than depleted in litigation; Virginia's health stabilized; and the sons began to experience a less tense relationship with their mother and she with them, although not free from tension and difficulties. It seems that Virginia attained her goal of distributing her assets as she saw fit while also "achieving some level of peace with her sons before she died." What the future will bring to this family is uncertain, but without doubt, they developed, even if so slightly, more capacity to deal with their differences.

Lessons Learned

Several lessons can be learned from this engagement. First, that decisions about wealth in families touch on a sensitive emotional chord for family members. Such sensitivities have their roots in the history of the family and are the foundation of many future

An Asset Distribution Plan that Produced Family Acrimony

difficulties. Learning about the multigenerational past gives the professional a perspective as he/she addresses the present problems related to wealth. The lawyer in this case obtained an understanding of the "irrational" responses of his client and of her sons only after learning about the family history.

Second, the way the professional approaches a family is crucial in defining the results of the engagement. Being objective and neutral is of the essence, yet it is a position easily compromised by the professional's own emotionality. This lawyer was able to attain a good outcome by being aware of his own emotional reactions.

Third, the professional plays a role in favoring the family's capacity to think clearly in the midst of the agitation, and thus favors better decision making. The lawyer helped Virginia's family go from a state of anxiety in which upset, anger and hurt prevailed, to a state where she and her sons could assess reality, communicate, and adjust their positions in favor of a better outcome.

Last, it is crucial to have an assessment of the degree of volatility of relationships within the family. This informs the professional as to which is the best approach to family meetings, including who, how, and when to contact the different family members involved in the consultation. In this case the lawyer knew that direct conversations between family members were necessary, but he also knew that premature meetings could push the family to the edge and over. He skillfully prepared the ground by regulating contact until productive family conversations were possible.

Key Takeaways

- Be aware that decisions about family wealth taps on the emotional life of the family.
- Learn about the history of the family. It provides information for understanding the present problem.
- Develop relationships with all family members involved in a situation.
- Clarify goals. The first and immediate request form a client might be in conflict with deeper goals that have to do with family relationships.
- Work to reduce the anxiety in the family. A less anxious family can make better decisions.
- Focus on the facts ("when," "who", "how," "when") rather than on the question "why."
- Estimate the level of chronic anxiety in the family system to determine strategy and interventions.
- Identify relationship triangles and use them to help the family attain their goals.

CHAPTER 3

A CHANGE OF DIRECTION AT THE EDGE OF THE CLIFF

A sister and brother in business together had one last chance to avoid legal and financial disaster. Problems within their business, with other family members, and with personal finances required them to make difficult decisions. What problem to address first? How to deal with the way emotional reactions obstructed possible solutions? How to interrupt the repetition of relationship patterns that had become an obstacle to progress?

Background

Jane and Charlie were sister and brother beneficiaries of a family trust (the "Trust") established by their grandfather. They were both licensed real estate brokers in the state where they resided and worked. Each had worked for other real estate firms before they had agreed to start their own brokerage several years ago. Jane was responsible for the management and finances of the firm, while Charlie handled marketing and other aspects of the firm's operations. The business was very successful and, combined with the addition of the Trust distributions, both Jane and Charlie received a substantial annual cash flow.

The Family

Jane maintained an extravagant lifestyle. She had private club memberships and season tickets to all local sports franchises. She owned an expensive oceanfront vacation property. Each of her three children was in either private colleges or private secondary school. Except for the oceanfront property, Jane had borrowed against her properties to the maximum degree possible. She had also incurred substantial amounts of unsecured debt. She had done all of this to maintain her lifestyle.

After some time, Jane had exhausted the cash available to her from the Trust. Without Charlie's knowledge, she had then borrowed against the brokerage's escrow account, which held client funds and money deposited by third parties for the brokerage to hold on their account. These funds were intended to be used as purchase deposits and other financial transactions. Jane used that borrowed escrow money for lifestyle purposes. In time, she began to reel from one cash crisis to another. Despite this, she made no effort to change her behavior.

Increasingly desperate, Jane borrowed $2.6 million from their Aunt A. Jane instructed her lawyer to draft the promissory note for this transaction, which did not contain customary remedies and lender protections, including indemnification rights. There is no record of Jane advising Aunt A to seek an independent counsel to represent her in these transactions. This is significant because Jane managed Aunt A's financial affairs for some period prior to borrowing from her. Within a few months thereafter, Aunt A's health deteriorated to the extent that a power of attorney she had given to her second husband was activated. After that, Aunt A was largely confined to her home where she received 24-hour nursing care, suffering from early-stage dementia, among other ailments.

Jane made no payments on the note made in favor of Aunt A for some time, despite the terms of the note. In the course of trying to become more involved in managing Aunt A's financial affairs, her second husband learned of the existence of the note and grew furious with Jane's conduct. He demanded payment of the note, but Jane was unable to pay. On behalf of Aunt A, the step-uncle filed suit against Jane not only for nonpayment of the note, but also alleging that there was a relationship of trust and confidence Jane had with her Aunt A that Jane had breached.

Jane also owed a substantial amount to the IRS because she had under-withheld income taxes in order to have additional cash for her personal needs.

As the walls were closing in, Jane reluctantly told Charlie of her actions. Charlie was momentarily panicked. First, he was advised that Jane's conduct regarding the borrowing from their aunt might constitute a crime under the laws of the jurisdiction where Aunt A lived. Even if it were not a criminal offense, any civil judgment against Jane would significantly damage his sister's reputation and thus, the reputation of their brokerage.

Second, Charlie realized that if the money Jane had taken from the brokerage's escrow account was not restored quickly, it could cause her, and perhaps the brokerage as well, to lose their licenses. In short, almost any of these adverse outcomes would likely destroy the brokerage and all that Jane and he had built. It was also likely that his reputation would be damaged as well.

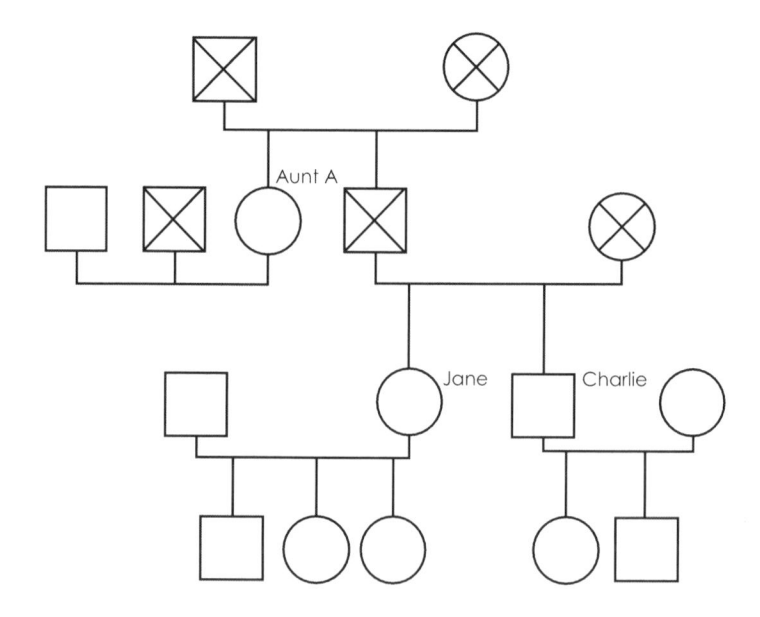

The Engagement

The matter was referred to a family business lawyer by a financial advisor who was a friend of Jane and aware of the relevant history. The lawyer met with both Jane and Charlie, who jointly agreed to retain the lawyer to deal with the issues that directly and indirectly impacted the brokerage, including the lawsuit filed by their step-uncle.

Jane did most of the talking during the initial meeting. She was mostly defensive and largely avoided accepting any responsibility for the complex web of problems the siblings faced. Charlie was quieter, but when he interjected, it was to emphasize the importance of directly and effectively addressing the problems. At no point during that meeting did he appear angry toward Jane or express any blame toward her.

Insight:

Financial stress is a powerful source of anxiety. When anxiety is heightened, people are less capable of assessing reality and responding accordingly and there is less capacity to look at one's behavior objectively. These qualities characterized Jane's reactions during the meeting. Charlie was more matter of fact and solution-focused. He was more capable of containing the anxiety that such an extreme circumstance produced and better able to look at the problem dispassionately.

Several meetings with both Jane and Charlie followed. These meetings were devoted to a review of the history of Jane's financial distress and family disputes. These meetings included extensive discussions of each sibling's goals, which were potentially in conflict. Jane was principally concerned with the preservation of her image and status among friends and business associates. Under the circumstances, this concern led Jane to suggest one course of action after another to avoid any public acknowledgment of her financial distress, regardless of the consequence to Charlie or the brokerage.

On the other hand, Charlie was less preoccupied with his image but valued the continuation of the brokerage most highly.

For Charlie the brokerage represented the achievement and culmination of not only his life's work but Jane's as well. It was made explicit to the siblings that they needed to be mindful that the discrepancy in their priorities represented the potential for conflict, and that they should work on ways to accommodate each other's goals. Ultimately both wanted to maintain both their relationship and their partnership.

The last of these meetings concluded with a request that Jane gather and transmit to the lawyer all documents, promissory notes, loan applications, correspondence, and any other relevant records for review and analysis. Jane gathered several hundred pages of records and produced them. The records revealed that Jane was teetering on the edge of bankruptcy. This was confirmed by Jane's financial advisor who had prepared several sophisticated financial models that indicated that, under the best of circumstances, Jane could continue for several months at most before being required to seek protection from her creditors.

The records also indicated that Jane's actual outstanding obligation to the IRS exceeded the original estimate. Additionally, there was a deeply acrimonious relationship between Jane and her step-uncle, with mutual accusations of undue influence and other illegal conduct.

The Professional's Evaluation and Interventions

Assembling a team

At this point, it was the consensus of the advisors, Charlie, and Jane (grudgingly), that a team should be formed. It would include the parties, the lawyer, the financial advisor, an accountant with experience negotiating settlements with the IRS, and bankruptcy counsel. These experts were needed to formulate a plan and strategy for all issues involving Jane and the brokerage.

Also, in private, Charlie retained a family systems consultant to help him understand the family's emotional dynamic, how it had contributed to creating the current crisis, and in what ways it might be impeding their attempts to find a solution to the present conundrum. He was interested in managing the family relationship aspect of the problem as best he could.

Addressing the different perspectives

As the team worked with the siblings, it became clear that their perspectives on how to solve the problems were fundamentally different. Jane seemed far less prepared to genuinely accept that her financial status was dire, while Charlie was more realistic about how extreme their situation was. He also understood that immediate measures were required. Jane was particularly critical of Charlie's conclusion, though shared by all of their professional advisors, that Jane needed to consider bankruptcy immediately. She considered bankruptcy an admission of personal and financial failure, as well as an event that was going to harm her professionally. It was evident Jane wanted to avoid bankruptcy at almost any cost. Charlie considered Jane's bankruptcy as the only realistic option for getting out of the "swamp."

In the matter of the unpaid note to Aunt A, Charlie advocated for a settlement with their step-uncle. He argued that there was no doubt that a debt was due, and any outcome other than a settlement jeopardized the future of the brokerage. Jane wanted to vigorously contest the step-uncle because she not only felt aggrieved by her step-uncle's accusations but wanted to counter-sue as well.

Insight:

People often fall into a pattern of making choices directed to alleviate the pain of the moment, while disregarding longer-term consequences. This happens when the intellect is flooded by emotionality in such a way that decisions are guided by what "feels right" rather than by what "is necessary." Over the years, Jane (and Charlie, to a lesser degree) had fallen into a pattern of handling problems by finding short-term solutions at the expense of long-term stability. At this point, this strategy was unsustainable if they wanted a chance at fixing their problems. It would require a big effort on the part of both to begin to modify this pattern.

Having different opinions was somewhat new between Jane and Charlie. Historically, Charlie had agreed with Jane on almost everything, particularly in issues relating to the finances of the business. As the current crisis became more complicated, Charlie communicated that he no longer trusted Jane's decision-making. He also was very concerned about the way she was addressing the problem. Jane did not appreciate Charlie's point of view. She was often not only in disagreement, but openly disrespectful of Charlie in team meetings. At one point, there was a discussion about the potential criminal liability Jane faced, and a team member asked Charlie for his opinion about a potential strategy. Jane snapped, "Don't ask him; this is my life, not his."

A Change of Direction at the Edge of the Cliff

While most of the team agreed with Charlie in his perspective, the lawyer believed it was very important never to discount or be dismissive of Jane's point of view, even when that perspective seemed irrational. For example, Jane articulated a number of times that she thought she might be able to reschedule all of her debt. Because of this, she continued to pursue several financiers. No other member of the team had a positive reaction to this course of action, and in fact, the members of the team who were financial professionals prepared analyses that conclusively showed that rescheduling the debt, was it even possible, would only worsen Jane's financial prospects long-term. Nonetheless, the lawyer encouraged Jane to pursue whatever steps she thought possible, so long as she supported progress and movement on other fronts.

In short, in contrast with the past when Charlie had deferred to Jane, he was now determined to be part of the decision-making. When he voiced his concerns, they were often in conflict. A level of consensus was required if they wanted to have a chance for survival. Accordingly, individual work with each sibling was needed to help them explore options.

The strategy

After months of discussion, the consensus (with Jane objecting in some part) was that three steps should be taken. The first, was that Jane should plan for a bankruptcy filing. Out of respect for her belief that she might be able to "make something happen" financially in the interim, however, the siblings' lawyer suggested that the possibility that this filing could be averted be left open.

The second, was that Jane's oceanfront property would be sold since this was the only property in which Jane had equity. The first portion of the proceeds would be used to retire the IRS debt. Bankruptcy counsel indicated that any IRS debt would not be dischargeable in a bankruptcy proceeding, and so it was important that it be addressed before any filing.

The third, was that all efforts possible be taken to resolve the lawsuit filed by the step-uncle, including the use of the remainder of the proceeds from the property to fashion a settlement.

Addressing the lawsuit

On behalf of Jane, the siblings' lawyer contacted the lawyer who represented the step-uncle and had filed the lawsuit. That conversation confirmed that the relationship between his client and Jane had deteriorated to the extent that his client did not trust Jane to any degree. That lawyer also indicated that Jane made statements to the step-uncle that the step-uncle regarded as at best misleading if not false, statements that they interpreted as attempts to delay the filing of the suit. Also, the lawyer indicated that he (the lawyer) had multiple communications directly with Jane that left him with the same impression. The level of distrust was so deep that the lawyer frankly did not believe that Jane's financial status was dire, and made it clear he would not change his view unless strong evidence to the contrary was provided. It was clear to the siblings' lawyer that some level of trust between Jane and her step-uncle had to be restored to make any progress.

The siblings' lawyer had extensive conversations with the step-uncle's lawyer, including one face-to-face lengthy lunch. The purpose of that lunch was not only to further communication but also to attempt to build some professional trust between Jane's lawyer and himself. Since they were agents for their respective clients, building trust between them could in a sense constitute the restoration of some trust between their clients. Trust did develop between the lawyers, as they maintained frequent (no less often than weekly) contact, which uniformly began with some discussion about events in their personal and professional lives. When there was tension and conflict between them, it was quickly resolved. At one point, the siblings' lawyer misinterpreted a communication, called the step-uncle's lawyer to confront him about it, and the step-uncle's lawyer hung up on him. When the siblings' lawyer realized his error, he immediately called the step-uncle's lawyer to apologize, and the step-uncle's lawyer cut him off, saying, "I know who you are and realized you must have misread what I wrote. Don't worry about it." This reaction would not have been possible without the relationship they had been working on for some time.

At the conclusion of their first lunch, the step-uncle's lawyer asked that Jane provide any financial records and/or analysis which supported the claim that Jane could not realistically expect to avoid bankruptcy. Jane did so shortly thereafter. Upon receiving the records, the lawyer called and asked for permission to speak with Jane's bankruptcy counsel. As part of the continuing effort to improve communications and build trust, the siblings' lawyer granted that authority. Bankruptcy counsel confirmed that he had prepared a draft petition and was ready to file at the appropriate time.

Seeing the Blind Spot

Insight:

Professionals working with families become "temporary family members" in the sense that, as is the case with any other member, their behavior and approach affect others in the group. When professionals are tense, unsure, belligerent, or upset, they affect the whole family environment and feed into the already existing tensions. When professionals take a more dispassionate and rational position, the whole group calms down, allowing them to then move toward a realistic solution to problems.

Months of negotiations followed between the siblings' lawyer and the lawyer for the step-uncle in an effort to identify a resolution that would be agreeable to the step-uncle and would provide Jane (and Charlie) with what was most important to them: the dismissal of the lawsuit, or at least dismissal of the count that alleged wrongful conduct by Jane.

One solution after another was discussed and discarded. Finally, the siblings' lawyer took Jane aside and persuaded her that it would be beneficial if they could provide a proposal that unmistakably reflected her desire to benefit her aunt. One of the obstacles was that Jane was no longer dealing directly with her Aunt A but was dealing with her step-uncle as Aunt A's agent. Jane detested the step-uncle and held him responsible for the absence of any direct contact between her and Aunt A.

Jane's feelings toward him affected her willingness to make that type of proposal, so there were multiple discussions before she was able to do so. The result was that the siblings' lawyer obtained Jane's consent to communicate to the step-uncle's lawyer that while Jane was heading toward bankruptcy, she genuinely wanted to benefit Aunt A as much as possible. Therefore, they proposed that Jane would issue a new promissory note in the amount then outstanding, which with interest at that time totaled just over $2.8 million. The note would provide that Jane would assign to Aunt A, Jane's right to that portion of the proceeds from the sale of the oceanfront property that was in excess of all outstanding tax obligations. The excess was just over $800,000 and would constitute a partial prepayment of the new replacement promissory note.

There was risk that the assignment of the $800,000 from the oceanfront proceeds would be set aside in bankruptcy as an insider preference because of the family relationship between Jane and Aunt A, and so the siblings' lawyer further proposed that if all or any part of the $800,000 prepayment was in fact "clawed back" in bankruptcy, that clawed-back amount would be added back to the principal amount of the note. This arrangement would mean that if Jane declared bankruptcy and the prepayment was in fact clawed back, Aunt A would be no worse off than had the transaction not been consummated. On the other hand, if the prepayment was not challenged in bankruptcy, Aunt A would receive substantially more than if she only received some portion of Jane's bankruptcy estate.

The step-uncle accepted the proposal. The communication through his lawyer that Jane was genuinely trying to help Aunt A achieve a better result – and was matched by a proposal that would give her a much better result than if Jane had left her to be an unsecured creditor in bankruptcy – was identified by the step-uncle's lawyer as an event that helped move the step-uncle to agreement.

Insight:

The lawyers, who had now developed a working relationship based on mutual trust and respect, were able to move to a more creative platform considering real facts and real possibilities. The fluid communication between the lawyers also made it possible for their clients to alleviate earlier suspiciousness about each other. The lawyers' intervention calmed the situation to the point that both Jane and the step-uncle were open to considering a compromise as a solution.

Charlie's realization

While deeply dismayed by Jane's conduct, Charlie realized that he had played a role in creating the risk the brokerage faced by not being more engaged. He also had not made enough effort to educate himself about the decisions Jane was making. Based on his consultation with the counselor on family systems, he moved toward realistically recognizing the part he played in creating and sustaining the problem and identified steps he needed to take to modify his participation.

Insight:

Everybody involved in a family problematic situation plays a part in creating and sustaining it. It seems that the more Jane concealed the reality of their financial situation, the more Charlie avoided learning about it. One did the hiding; the other averted his eyes. In this sense, both contributed to the problem.

Furthermore, Charlie acknowledged that he had benefitted from some of Jane's decisions that he now viewed as mistakes. For example, part of Jane's lifestyle was to throw lavish parties. Some of those who attended became staple clients of the brokerage, and Charlie had to admit that some of the financial rewards he received over the years were due to Jane's lifestyle choices.

Charlie also realized that his style of conflict avoidance had prevented him from expressing his point of view to his sister. He said he avoided acting when he wanted to proceed in a certain direction for fear of a confrontation. He recognized it was very uncomfortable for him to deal with her when she was upset. In short, caving in and accommodating to his sister had been a costly strategy for the sake of keeping the peace and maintaining his comfort.

As a result of realizing the part he had played in creating the present problem, Charlie was determined to change the way he had been participating in the business for the past years. He was prepared to restore the amount Jane took from the firm's escrow fund from his personal assets, but only if Jane shared control of the firm's financial affairs and other significant governance matters with him. Seeing no other alternative, Jane reluctantly agreed.

Insight:

A family is a system. Therefore, a change in one individual affects other individuals in the group. Charlie's determination to become more involved with the business affected Jane. As new behavior is introduced, even if the change is considered positive, it usually encounters a reaction in the shape of opposition, criticism, or push-back. When Charlie decided to become more involved and take on new responsibilities, Jane resisted and attempted to have Charlie go back to his "old position." It remains to be seen if Charlie can sustain his new behavior long enough to make it a permanent change.

The Aftermath

Within six weeks of consummating the transaction with Aunt A and Charlie restoring the amount taken from the escrow account, Jane filed for bankruptcy. The trustee in bankruptcy did not attempt to undo the new transaction with his step-uncle on behalf of Aunt A, or to recover the $800,000 paid to Aunt A with proceeds from the oceanfront property. Despite this, there was no indication that the relationship between Aunt A and Jane would be reestablished. She and her step-uncle remain estranged.

The brokerage survived. The new shared management of the brokerage was uncomfortable for both Jane and Charlie and led to some serious conflicts. Jane was never entirely happy with the loss of control over the brokerage that these events caused. Also, her lifestyle was dramatically altered including the loss of her private club memberships and season tickets. She was still trying to adjust to living more modestly.

The underlying value conflict between Jane and Charlie remained and flared up from time to time, manifesting itself in differences over strategy in the brokerage, how much of its profit to distribute, and similar issues. Up to the ending of the present consultation, their relationship as siblings was sustained to a reasonable degree.

Commentary on the Emotional Aspect of the Process

The present case illustrates four aspects in the professional consultation that are impacted by emotions and relationships. It also identifies ways in which professionals can maneuver in order to provide the services they were retained for. These are a) Achieving communication between parties that are not able to collaborate (*Building bridges and developing trust*), b) Moving the family from an emotionally-driven decision-making style to a more thoughtful way of addressing problems led by one member in the family and helped by realistic professionals (*From emotionality to thoughtfulness*), c) Knowing that everybody plays a part in the creation and maintenance of a problem (*Everybody plays a part*), and d) Considering the client's values and principles in the consultation process (*Keeping values and principles top of mind*).

Building bridges and developing trust

At the onset of this consultation, the relationship between Jane and her step-uncle had been severely damaged to the point that personal interactions were impossible. The relationship was so characterized by mistrust, mostly rooted in the step-uncle's conclusion that, in substance, Jane had taken advantage of Aunt A, that reaching a settlement of the disputes over the unpaid debt was severely hampered. Any resolution required the restoration of some element of trust, at least enough to permit discussion and negotiation. Trust is developed through continuous contact and honest interest about the perspective and well-being of the other. Also, trust is developed through congruency between words and actions, and with predictable behavior. The relationship between

Jane and her step-uncle was so affected that directly introducing any of these elements to rebuild trust was almost impossible. The only option was for the lawyer to function as a bridge between them.

The siblings' lawyer's first task was to connect with their step-uncle. He did this through the step-uncle's lawyer. It required a display of openness in order to create enough trust to begin a productive dialogue. He did this by being transparent about Jane's financial situation, by offering the information needed to substantiate his statements, by clearing any doubts the other party had, and by establishing a professional and amicable relationship. It took time and continuous contact.

The relationship between the lawyers made possible an indirect exchange between Jane and her step-uncle, and in a way between Jane and Aunt A. After extensive conversations with Jane, her lawyer helped her communicate to the step-uncle (through the lawyer himself) that Jane had Aunt A's best interest in mind, and that she was determined to back her interest with concrete action. It was only then that the step-uncle was open to considering options other than the lawsuit.

The quality of the exchange between the lawyers, who were representing the family members at opposite sides, was key in avoiding the lawsuit. At the onset, each lawyer brought with him the animosity from their respective clients. As the lawyers developed a working relationship and tension dissipated between them, they reached a point where they could lower their guard, put aside the anger and suspicion transmitted by each of their clients, and focus on the task of finding a favorable resolution. After almost eight months of regular conversations, they were able to creatively devise a solution.

When professionals engage with a family they become, in a sense, part of that family. It is as if they are "temporary family members." In this capacity, when professionals can relate to others in a calm and thoughtful way, the whole group has an opportunity to also calm down and raise their functioning. The way professionals approach the family problem has an impact on the increasing or decreasing of the tension in the family group. This said, the first task of a professional is to help lower the anxiety in the family in relation to the issue at hand. The lawyer's approach to Jane and Charlie was serene and matter of fact, and his approach to the step-uncle—through his lawyer—was direct and relaxed. His presence and demeanor contributed to reducing tensions in the system as a whole.

The lawyer's effort yielded good results. He diligently worked first to develop a professional relationship between him and the step-uncle's lawyer, and then, indirectly, to develop some level of trust between Jane and the step-uncle. The compromise that Jane and the step-uncle reached would have been unlikely without the restoration of some degree of confidence between the two.

From emotionality to thoughtfulness

No single action led Jane and Charlie to the delicate situation they found themselves in. It represented the snowball effect of a series of choices over many years. It is very difficult to judge what is a good or a poor decision in the very moment of making a choice. A rule of thumb is that unsound decisions are often guided by impulses rather than by careful thinking. Decisions that are made based on emotions, i.e. automatic or instinctual, are generally directed toward alleviating the discomfort of the moment. On the other hand, decisions based on the intellect are informed by emotions but are not governed by the pressure of the immediate discharge of tension. For example, Jane's financial risk-taking seems to have been driven more by her anxiety about how her image would be affected if she trimmed her lifestyle, than by carefully thinking about the long-term impact of her actions.

Everybody is subject to the power of emotionality to different degrees. Emotionally-driven lives represent a way of living directed to maintaining the short-term equilibrium to the detriment of long-term stability. It is as if Jane and Charlie conducted themselves with the purpose of minimizing the discomfort in the present with little regard for the future outcome. Jane might have experienced discomfort from not fulfilling a set of perceived social expectations, and Charlie might have experienced discomfort from upsetting Jane through confrontation or difference of opinion. For example, Jane preferred to continue her private club memberships even when the cost was beyond her means, to avoid what she saw as social embarrassment. Charlie preferred to be disengaged from the financial matters of the brokerage rather than upsetting Jane. Some people have more sensitivity to perceived acceptance and love from others and are more prone to fulfilling their expectations and avoiding their upsets. As illustrated by this case, perceived love, expectations, and upsets are powerful forces that shape behavior.

The lawyer recognized the power of the emotions that were stirred as Jane and Charlie faced their dire financial and legal

A Change of Direction at the Edge of the Cliff

situation. Understanding the emotional forces helped him pace his interventions and to be understanding of their deep struggle. He could have been more aggressive in his interventions because there was little doubt about what was required. Nevertheless, the lawyer was patient, especially with Jane who in numerous occasions attempted to undo mutual decisions and wanted to go back to her previous style of addressing problems. For example, in the face of imminent bankruptcy, she continued to come up with ideas about how to reschedule her debt, even when financial evidence provided by professionals showed it was impossible.

Often, it is not until families face an extreme situation that they realize they have to shift from their emotionally-oriented life style to a more thoughtful-oriented one. Frequently this realization comes too late, and the consequences on wealth, businesses, and relationships are devastating. Yet, other times families rise to the occasion and develop new ways of functioning. Jane and Charlie, more by force than by choice, began to make modifications to their approach to decision-making. They needed the assistance of a team of professionals to help them face a reality they were avoiding, and to make the necessary adjustments to modify course. Jane and Charlie benefitted from the firmness and grounding of all professionals involved, each providing an objective evaluation in their field of expertise.

A family group that moves toward more thoughtfulness is usually led by one individual. Such a leader, rather than telling others what to do, makes changes to his/her behavior to become the most responsible person he/she can be. Leadership comes through determination to walk in a certain direction, often facing other's criticism and even rejection. If this person can sustain the effort long enough, others begin to raise their functioning as well, and the upset subsides. In this case, Charlie was determined to re-take his responsibilities as owner of the brokerage which he had surrendered for many years. He also decided to assume the costs of mistakes of the past by paying off the borrowed money from the business escrow. He increased his capacity to tolerate the uncomfortable confrontations with Jane in favor of longer-term benefits. These shifts represented a more mature position and had the potential for bringing the family along to a higher level of functioning. In a sense, he invited everybody to be slightly more thoughtful and less subject to repeating the problematic patterns of the past. It remains to be seen if Charlie can sustain his determination over time. It also remains to be seen if Jane can move in that direction as well.

Everybody plays a part

It is all too easy to blame Jane for the profound problems these siblings had. That would be an inaccurate analysis of a much more complicated reality. A problem such as the one described in this engagement does not develop overnight. It requires the long-term active participation of all the individuals involved. Jane contributed by pretending, hiding information, and utilizing risky and inadequate strategies to maintain an artificial standard of living. Charlie contributed by playing along, by being disengaged from aspects of the business he owned, and by not questioning Jane in the face of evidence that things were not right. The problem evolved from a series of reciprocal interactions.

It is a challenge to keep in mind reciprocity in relationships because there is an inclination to identify a guilty party and point at his/her faulty behavior. More sophisticated professionals can see multiple sides of a problem and appreciate how everybody contributes to its creation and maintenance. This point of view also allows them to see how everybody can be part of the solution. The advantage of this perspective is that it helps professionals be matter of fact, realistic, and avoid blaming and casting guilt, which rarely have a constructive effect. In this case, knowledge about reciprocity in relationships provided professionals a rationale for sustaining an impartial position when relating to the siblings. It helped them keep the focus on the possible solutions.

Keeping values and principles top of mind

Jane and Charlie were not only business partners, they were also and foremost, siblings. Pressures such as the ones experienced by these siblings have the potential to disrupt family ties, resulting in a relationship chasm that is difficult to overcome. Jane and Charlie valued sharing many aspects of their lives beside their work, including the relationship between their two nuclear families. They liked to spend celebrations and vacations together, and they cherished the relationship their children had as cousins. They knew that the business financial crisis was a threat to their personal relationship, but it was Charlie who communicated more of a concern about a possible distancing or rupture as the result of this crisis. In his interventions, the lawyer had in mind that his clients' goal was not only to solve their financial and legal problem, but to stay together in business and maintain their sibling relationship.

Jane and Charlie did not share all of each other's values. Nevertheless, they both held the value of "family unity and well-being" as a priority. Often, other values each of them held as important conflicted with this fundamental value, and conversations were necessary to re-establish an alignment. For example, Jane's value of her social status often jeopardized the relationship with her brother because in her efforts to protect her social image, she was hurting his financial wellbeing. Charlie had the value of openness and transparency, but if he freely shared his problems with the outside community, he would have damaged Jane's desire to keep a certain social image. The siblings had to find a way to honor their common values and respect each the values that were different. The lawyer had to keep in mind what was important for each person and for them as a team when considering possible solutions to their problems. For example, the lawyer knew that both siblings valued being in business together, therefore the option of solving the problem by dissolving the brokerage was not pursued.

Charlie, who somehow was able to be more serene, addressed the theme of values more directly. In private conversations he made explicit his determination to separate as much as possible his personal relationship with his sister from problems with the business. He made a point of not giving in to the anger and frustration he often experienced. He also made a point of sustaining direct and continuous contact with Jane, even in the face of disagreement. Finally, he determined to be open, transparent, and realistic with his own family about the situation, but without speaking poorly about Jane as a person or being critical of her.

Clarity about one's values is a way to maintain a direction in the midst of a crisis. Being explicit about what is important for self helps guide one's life based on principle rather than on the impulse of the moment. For Charlie, and to a lesser degree for Jane, the value they put into their relationship as siblings helped them navigate the crisis without totally eroding their relationship.

Final Comments

There is no certainty that Jane and Charlie will continue in business together in the future, or that they will be able to save their personal relationship after this blow. But certainly, by the end of this engagement, they had managed to survive this chapter in the life of their business and in their relationship. Brother and sister stepped up to the occasion as their lawyers gracefully helped them to walk the painful but necessary path that gave them the chance of a fresh start.

Lessons Learned

The present case offers some useful lessons when the future looks gloomy and disaster is rapidly approaching. This engagement made it very clear that the professional has the responsibility of abiding to reality, as difficult as reality might be. Therefore, the first lesson learned was that emotions get in the way of the client grasping the severity of a situation, but if the advisor is aware of these emotions he/she can facilitate the process. For Jane it was extremely difficult to accept her financial collapse and the legal predicament she faced, yet the lawyer gracefully but implacably helped her face the actual state of things.

The second lesson speaks about the relevance of building trust between professionals representing family members whose relationship is too eroded for direct contact. Jane's lawyer and aunt A's lawyer built a bridge that was likely the only opportunity to reach a workable solution to a problem that was attaining immense proportions with terrible consequences. Their open and direct relationship was the only route to collaboration.

Lastly, this case teaches how a family, led by one member, can move from an emotionally guided life style to a more thoughtful approach. Jane and her brother Charlie, forced by their dire situation, began to inch away from unquestionable disaster in their financial, legal, and family life, to salvaging their finances, their relationship and their business. Recovery was guided by clear principles and determination, particularly from Charlie.

Key Takeaways

- Be aware that the professionals become part of the family system, and their participation has the potential of calming down or increasing tension within the group.

- Restore trust between opposing parties through open, honest communication. Trust is based on congruency between words and actions, predictability, and on legitimate interest in the wellbeing of the other as reflected by actions.

- Promote movement toward more thoughtfulness and less emotionality. It can make a big difference in the kind of decisions that people make.

A Change of Direction at the Edge of the Cliff

- Identify a family leader. A family member who decides to take steps to becoming the most responsible person he/she can be can lead the group in a new direction.

- Don't give up when faced with push-back. Change in one individual usually encounters a reaction from other members in a family system.

- Clarify and make values and principles explicit. They represent the compass in the midst of the crisis.

CHAPTER 4

BUSINESS PROBLEMS AND FAMILY PROBLEMS INTERTWINED

This case concerns a tense and troubled relationship between a father and son that was rooted in part on events that happened in previous generations. At the start of the engagement, events were pushing them into open and perhaps protracted conflict.

Background

When the engagement described below began, Paul Robertson was a 67-year old man who was the Chairman and CEO of a company that designed and manufactured signal processing equipment (the "Family Business"). The engagement related to Paul's retention of lawyer regarding conflicts that arose in the Family Business and in Paul's family.

The Family

Paul's father, Harold, had been an irascible but brilliant innovator who developed many valuable electronic technologies that were used effectively by the U.S. Navy for espionage and other operations during World War II. Paul's relationship with Harold had always been characterized by a great degree of tension. Paul had one younger brother, Michael, who had died several years ago as a consequence of substance abuse. As tense as Paul's relationship had been with Harold, Michael's had been worse: Michael and Harold had become estranged when Michael was in his early twenties, and the two never reconciled.

Harold died more than twenty years ago, but one aspect of the conflict between father and son lived on. When Paul was a teenager, Harold began an extramarital affair with a woman, Sara. The affair progressed, and Harold left Paul's mother to marry Sara. Sara had two children from a previous marriage. The two families never quite blended, and Paul had an uneasy relationship with not only Sara but with his step-siblings, Samuel and Myrna. Paul would later acknowledge that he felt bitterness toward both his father and Sara over the effect of their actions on his mother who had been cast aside and struggled after the divorce.

Paul's wife, Margaret, had died several years earlier. He had not re-married. He had two children. The older child, John, 39, worked as the Vice President of Sales for the Family Business. The younger child, Diana, 35 was not involved in the Family Business. She was a stay-at-home mother but remained significantly financially dependent on her father.

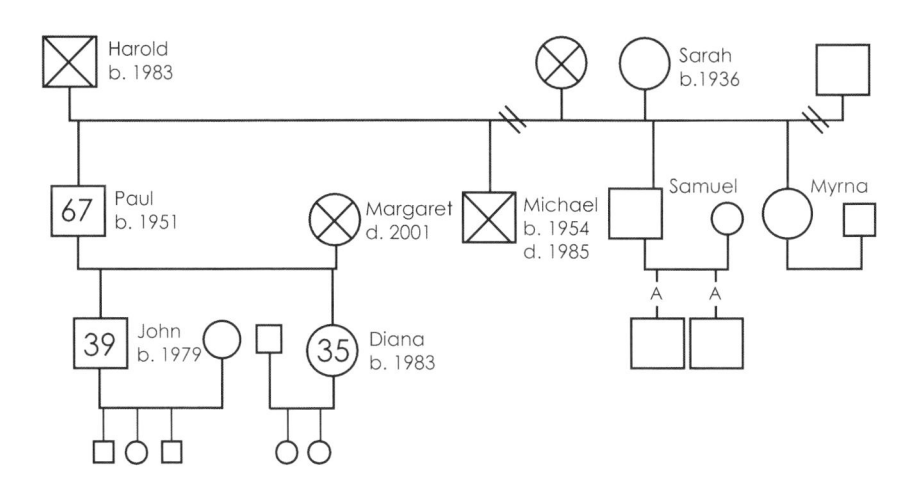

Business Problems and Family Problems Intertwined

Paul's relationship with John was complicated. The two got along sometimes, but often experienced a conflict that lead to little or no contact for many months. As a result, their relationship was guarded and often distant. This had been their pattern for many years. Paul was closer with Diana, but they occasionally experienced conflicts that led to communications interruptions too.

Insight:

A recurring theme for the Robertson family is the use of distance as a way to deal with relationship tensions. From Harold and his affair, to Paul and his interruption of communications with his children, moving away from one another, rather than dealing with difficulties up front, has been an ongoing behavior. Creating space to deal with differences is an automatic reaction in families. It is useful and adaptive as it helps release tension. Yet, when the use of distance becomes chronic, it turns out to be less useful and creates a new set of problems in addition to the one that first led to the distance.

The Family Business was started by Harold after his return from the war and Paul had worked for him for many years. In his will, Harold left equal shares of the Family Business to Paul and Sara, creating a forced coexistence that deepened the already awkward relationship between the two.

The equipment designed and manufactured by the Family Business was sold principally to telecommunications companies. The Family Business held some patents related to signal processing designs and related purposes. It had an excellent reputation due to its long-standing technological innovation.

Paul led the Family Business for a long period following Harold's death, while Sara (who at the time of the professional engagement was 82) had always stayed in the shadows. Five years before this engagement, Paul had stepped away from full-time work at the Family Business and was contemplating "full" retirement. There were two seats on the Board of Directors, one held by Paul and one held by Sara, but the reality was that there had been no Board meetings in several years, as neither member desired to engage with one another in that manner. The Family Business largely kept running through its own momentum and, in recent years, through the efforts of John, which had been very energetic and valuable.

The Engagement

Paul had nearly completed his estate planning, and his estate planning lawyer believed Paul needed additional advice and services regarding the Family Business. His estate planner was concerned

Business Problems and Family Problems Intertwined

over two issues. The first was whether Paul could plan on the continuation of distributions from the Family Business that would be large enough to fund his lifestyle during his retirement. While Paul had other assets, they were largely illiquid, and Paul was dependent on distributions from the Family Business not only to sustain his own lifestyle but also to support Diana. The second concern was Paul's intention to leave his portion of the Family Business stock equally to John and Diana. The estate planner asked Paul to analyze that intention further, particularly with a focus on John's actions in starting ventures that could be interpreted as competitive with the Family Business. Paul engaged a corporate lawyer who also had experience in dealing with family businesses, to advise him regarding both issues.

Paul

After being engaged, the lawyer's first meeting was with Paul. Paul confided that in the five-year period since he had stepped away from the Family Business, he had largely been disengaged from the Family Business. He also candidly acknowledged that main reason for his disengagement was that the monthly distributions to him and Sara from the Family Business (which were well into five figures) were uninterrupted, and so neither he nor Sara had the incentive to intervene and confront John about the matters described in the next paragraph.

Paul disclosed that John had applied for and had been granted design patents in his name related to the designs the Family Business has protected. Further, Paul was aware that John had started another company, which was manufacturing and distributing products based on these design patents. There was no direct competition at that point between the Family Business and John's company, but the designs and products could be regarded as logical outgrowths of the Family Business. The possibility was that these actions violated duties and obligations John had to the Family Business. In Paul's view, the potential for John's company was vast; if John put his full-time attention to it, it could easily be valued at more than $50M in two years, about twice the value of the Family Business. At the end of the meeting, Paul floated the possibility of suing John for breach of his obligations to the Family Business. Paul not only felt angry and betrayed by John, but also was concerned for his own financial future.

Insight:

The way Paul disengaged from the Family Business for a long period of time and then came back to confront John about his behavior in relation to the business, echoes other instances in which members of this family used distance as a "style" of dealing with challenges, followed by a phase of confrontation and conflict creating cycles of tension – distance – conflict – closeness.

John

Paul's lawyer next talked with John, who initially was reluctant to meet with him. John's manner during the meeting was suspicious and defensive. John began by expressing his interest in managing the Family Business, but he also expressed anxiety over how his father was likely to handle the question of succession. First, John was not convinced that his father intended to pass down

Business Problems and Family Problems Intertwined

Paul's shares to John and Diana. If Paul did so, John believed that at minimum, he was entitled to a larger share in the Family Business than was Diana. Second, John expressed that his father could be very emotional, and thus made it difficult for John to be sure he could rely on him.

John acknowledged tension and occasional disconnects with his father. John's perspective was that much of the distrust resulted from what John refers to as "a serious mistake" he had made many years ago. After work one day, John went out to dinner with a few co-workers. John admitted that there was a great amount of drinking involved. On the way home, John struck a pedestrian, who suffered some significant physical injuries. John was arrested and charged with driving while intoxicated and assault and battery. It was a dire situation: John faced potential jail time if convicted. The family retained a local prominent criminal defense lawyer, who negotiated a plea agreement whereby John would plead no contest to a misdemeanor, receive a suspended sentence of one year, probation, and agree to pay all medical costs incurred by the pedestrian. Ultimately, Paul and Margaret paid all attorney costs and medical costs associated with this incident. While John expressed regret over his actions, he grew very angry when describing his parents' reaction to it, specifically the sense that after it they completely lost trust in him and treated him as a second-class citizen in his family. It was clear that the incident reverberated in the family.

Insight:
Stressful events in the life of a family are problematic not only because of the difficulties at the time of the event itself, but also due to the intensity of the reaction of family members to such

an event. This is exacerbated if the reaction persists over time such that a problem will not only result from the issue itself, but also from the continued reaction to it in the present.

Paul's lawyer concluded the interview by asking John about the patents that had been granted to him, and about his company. John turned very testy. In summary, John's position was that his company was selling different products in different markets and that no family member should have any right or claim to either the patents or to his company. John made it clear that if the succession planning did not produce a result that was acceptable to him, he would consider leaving the Family Business and devoting his full-time efforts to building his company. His direct quote was that "if it goes the wrong way, I'll just take my patents, products, customers, and go."

Diana

Even though Diana was not involved in the Family Business, Paul's lawyer decided to interview her to get her input. Diana confirmed that Paul and John have been at odds before John even reached the teenage years. As a result, Diana said that she sometimes felt "triangulated" between the two, often playing the role of peacemaker. Her view was that her father was often mercurial. She believed he had felt great pressure when she and John were younger, both of running the Family Business and running their family, as Margaret was a disengaged mother. There were many blowups between father and son.

Regarding John's arrest, Diana's perspective was that this event and related problems were evidence that her parents were willing

Business Problems and Family Problems Intertwined

to do anything for John, even welcoming him fully back into the Family Business after John displayed such immaturity and lack of judgment. She was resentful about that. She did concede, however, that John was an excellent salesman, and in her opinion, had vastly improved the sales and marketing efforts of the Family Business.

Diana indicated she felt conflicted because she felt inclined to support her brother and could understand why he may have felt he needed to protect himself by registering the patents and starting a new company. On the other hand, she was financially dependent on her father and understood why he may have felt threatened by John's actions. In short, she could see both sides of the issue but did have a financial interest in her father's point of view.

Insight:
Meeting with as many family members as possible gives the professional a wider perspective about the context of the presenting problem. Diana's input, even though she had not been involved in the Family Business, provided unique information about the family environment, which enriched the lawyer's understanding of the family dynamics.

The Professional's Evaluation and Interventions
John and his new business

The lawyer's first task was to analyze John's conduct regarding the patents and his formation of another company, and to advise Paul accordingly.

At the outset, a complication was that in the event action might have been warranted against John, Paul would have had to enlist Sara's agreement to any course as a matter of corporate law. Not only would approaching Sara in that manner be uncomfortable for Paul, but Sara seemed to be happy with John as long as the substantial distributions continued. This was a fact that Paul believed John understood and manipulated.

The documents that would bear on the analysis of John's conduct had to be carefully gathered, so that John was not alerted to the analysis and review that was taking place. Once those documents and other evidence was gathered, and the analysis done, the conclusion was that John's conduct was in a gray area, neither clearly legal nor clearly a violation of his obligations to the Family Business. The patents John registered were developed during the course of his employment by the Family Business. There was also evidence that he had used corporate resources to develop the patents. On the other hand, it appeared that the technologies and products to be sold in relation to the patents might be regarded as sufficiently distinct from the products of the Family Business. The bottom-line conclusion the lawyer reached was that any litigation over the issue (assuming Sara would support it) would be costly, very destructive to the Family Business and the family, and might not lead to a good result in any event.

> **Insight:**
> *Of paramount importance when advising families is getting as much factual information as possible, particularly in the face of events that elicit emotional responses, such as perceived threat, unfairness, disloyalty, being trapped or controlled. When people are upset, as Paul was, objectivity can be lost easily, and decisions are often made based on emotionally-informed*

conclusions. The thorough investigation done by the lawyer in relation to John's conduct was very important because it not only gave the lawyer the elements needed to make a judgment about the matter, but modified Paul's interpretation of John's behavior, toning the tension down.

The conclusion after evaluating John's conduct and his relationship with his father was that the issues between them would require time and patience to resolve. In conclusion, it would not be prudent at that moment to institute litigation as an attempt to address them. Since the succession plan with Sara might help resolve some of the issues between Paul and John and was necessary for the Family Business regardless, the lawyer decided instead to focus on that project next.

The succession plan

As noted, Sara at this stage was 82 years old. She was born into a family with substantial wealth, and by this point had a group of senior wealth management professionals who had the day-to-day responsibility of assisting her. Her long-time counsel represented her in connection with the succession plan. At first, he questioned the need for any succession planning for the Family Business, as in his words "everything had worked well to this point." After some reflection, however, he agreed that if the details could be worked out, it would be in both families' interest (Paul's and Sara's) if a provision was made for the transfer of each of their interest. He also stated that Sara, for sentimental reasons, wanted ownership of the Family Business to continue to be held by Harold's descendants and step-descendants, which would also argue in favor of a succession plan that allowed for transfer of stock in the Family Business among family members, but prohibited transfer to third parties without a right of first refusal.

Insight:

During calm times families often overlook difficulties that might emerge when circumstances change. In this case, Paul and Sara had not dealt with the issue of succession because it had not posed a challenge and they assumed it would be a smooth transition. When they gave the issue some thought, they identified potential pitfalls and decided to address the matter before it created problems. This is an example of the benefits of having an advisor who sees the bigger picture and who does not join the family in avoidance. The difficulties encountered in the succession planning process confirmed that it was indeed necessary to address it.

While it might have seemed that there should be few obstacles to coming to terms on a buy-sell agreement that incorporated the succession plan, the process proved to be contentious and emotional. Paul's lawyer came to believe that the origin of the problems went all the way back to at least as early as Sara's entrance into Paul's family, a conclusion that led him to favor slow, patient movement.

Almost every issue seemed to trigger some controversy. For example, even though she was a member of the Board of Directors, Sara really had very little idea of the operations or finances of the Family Business. As such, some education had to be provided in connection with the succession plan, so her counsel at one point reasonably asked that the Family Business produce its tax returns for the prior few years. When informed of this request, Paul erupted, demanding to know why she needed access to those tax returns. It required multiple sessions to calm Paul and get him to intercede with the controller of the Family Business to produce the tax returns. Paul seemed to resent any involvement by Sara in the Family Business. For her part, Sara also reacted emotionally to some developments in the negotiation. After some time, Paul's lawyer suggested to Sara's that unless absolutely necessary, their clients would be left off of email and other communications as virtually every one of them seemed to trigger some resentment or other issue that posed an obstacle to accomplishing what both Paul and Sara indicated they wanted.

Insight:
Quick and disproportionate reactions reveal a high level of ongoing tension in a family system, also referred to as chronic anxiety. It is the response to real or imagined threat to the well-being of its members, particularly to the disruption of relationships with important people. The abrupt way in which Harold's marriage ended, and the way Sara entered the family, were events that fueled the family's chronic anxiety. Such anxiety usually remains present decades, even generations, after the disruptive event itself. The pervasive high level of anxiety in this family was manifested, among other ways, in the volatility of the relationship between Paul and Sara.

A number of related family issues also complicated reaching agreement on the buy-sell agreement. Despite their many differences, Paul and John shared a personal and professional distaste for Samuel's two adopted children, whom they found lazy and spoiled.

Both Paul and John wanted to explore every means possible to keep them from inheriting any shares in the Family Business. After some discussions and failed efforts, it became apparent that there was no effective way to keep them from inheriting that would be acceptable to Sara, so Paul abandoned the issue.

Paul and Sara seemed to bear grievances from events that happened many years prior (Paul in how his mother had been treated, for which he partially blamed Sara, and Sara for Paul's unwillingness to accept her into his family) that were reflected in impulsive, emotional reactions to developments. For example, very late in the negotiations Sara's lawyer suggested there should be a sunset provision in the buy-sell agreement, meaning the agreement would terminate after some number of years. The suggestion was not irrational, but Paul – whose patience seemed to be quickly tried at every turn in the process – exploded and threatened to walk away from the discussions. Paul's counsel firmly reminded Paul of the benefits the agreement provided, how significant it would be to John and to a lesser degree Diana, and how self-destructive it would be to walk away. After a long night of reflection, Paul agreed, and the issue of a sunset clause was resolved.

Insight:
Paul's desire to walk away from the discussion seemed to be a purely emotional reaction rather than a well-considered decision. He benefitted from the lawyer's capacity to stay on track and firmly represent what he thought was best for his client. His firmness set the stage for Paul's reconsideration, his move toward viewing the situation more objectively, and his decision to finalize the succession agreement.

Business Problems and Family Problems Intertwined

Notwithstanding all of these obstacles, Paul and Sara ultimately were able to agree on the terms of a buy-sell agreement that provided a very basic framework for succession in the Family Business. John, who had been kept away from the discussions entirely, was surprised to learn of the agreement and was pleased to learn of its general contents, which Paul summarized for him. Reaching agreement represented a unique achievement in the family as, given their history and relationships, the members often found it difficult to cooperate effectively for any purpose.

Diana's financial crisis

Paul's lawyer then suggested that this was the time to turn their attention directly back to John, but at that moment, Diana experienced a financial crisis that had to be addressed. Diana and her husband (who worked as an alcohol and drug counselor), suddenly found themselves unable to meet their monthly obligations and turned to Paul to provide additional financial support to them. Paul, already stressed, turned to the lawyer. Neither Diana and her husband on the one hand, nor Paul on the other, could really explain why they faced the crisis. No one seemed to know where the money was going. The lawyer, who by this point had become Paul's trusted counselor, was asked to help the family find answers.

Insight:

A relationship pattern commonly seen in families, consists of one person becoming overly responsible for another, with the latter taking a less responsible position. This is referred to as the over/under-functioning pattern. Paul and Diana's way of handling their finances is a good example of this dynamic.

Paul had been providing Diana with financial support for an extended period of time, and Diana was not taking steps towards more financial autonomy. When the over/under-functioning pattern becomes fixed, it has detrimental consequences for both parties involved.

Paul's lawyer recruited an accountant to review the family's finances and determine why the crisis had occurred. The accountant was able to pinpoint multiple causes and held individual meetings with both Paul and Diana. He remarked to both that it "is unsustainable to live like this long-term, spending more money than is coming in." The statement awakened both Paul and Diana. After some additional work, the accountant suggested financial plans for both that allowed for very comfortable lifestyles but eliminated the extravagances that particularly characterized Diana's lifestyle.

One of the outcomes from the process was that Paul was forced to face that for many years he had enabled Diana to a degree that was self-destructive for him because he had neglected his own financial security in favor of subsidizing Diana's lifestyle. He had also discouraged her from taking steps to achieve greater financial independence. Paul seemed determined to address those factors. After discussions with the accountant and Diana, Paul decided he would reduce the amount he was giving to Diana monthly, but also provide her with a financial plan she could use to manage her own affairs, making such large distributions unnecessary. Paul indicated that this reduction alone removed some of the tension Paul said he felt toward John, because it relieved one source of the financial pressure Paul felt and therefore the need for the continued distributions in such a large amount from the Family Business.

Even though this process resulted in a smaller distribution to her from Paul, Diana adjusted. Diana decided she would get a job to help her family financially, a sign of independence and responsibility that gratified Paul. As part of the process, Diana became acquainted with Paul's lawyer and came to believe that even though he was representing Paul, he also was looking out for the family as a whole. She told John of her favorable impression.

Insight:
Paul and Diana benefitted from the input of the accountant, who offered a dispassionate evaluation of the situation and who helped them see the facts for what they were. This approach engaged the most "mature" side of both Paul and Diana in a way that allowed them to take steps toward responsibly addressing the problem and moving toward a long-term solution.

The lawyer becoming a resource for all family members while still representing Paul

The conversation between John and Diana about the lawyer led John to have second thoughts about some issues, specifically whether his reading of his father's intentions was entirely correct. Some of that reading came from his initial meeting with his father's lawyer. He knew that one purpose of the meeting had been so the lawyer could gather evidence relating to John's conduct, but he had also found the lawyer's demeanor in that meeting to be aggressive and adversarial. At that time John, representing the

Seeing the Blind Spot

Family Business, was starting discussions with representatives of the U.S. government about licensing some of its technologies. The transaction was potentially very significant to the Family Business and required much planning and organization. John decided he would try again with his father's lawyer by inviting his father and his father's lawyer to a planning and strategy meeting. The meeting went well and after, John called his father to thank him for his contributions and those made by his lawyer. John specifically commenting that Paul's lawyer "gets it." Subsequently, John directly called Paul's lawyer to apprise him of developments in negotiations over the licensing transaction.

Insight:

Intrinsic to interpersonal relationships is the use of triangles (a relationship among three people). Triangles can either amplify or reduce anxiety. Paul, John, and Diana formed a long-standing triangle characterized by tension in one, two, or three relationships (sides of the triangle). The lawyer was introduced, forming a set of interlocking triangles. The first intervention of the lawyer, when he approached John for the first time, seemed to intensify the tension between father and son. Presumably this happened because at that time the lawyer had taken the father's side. At a later time, the lawyer was able to maintain a more neutral position (even while serving as Paul's lawyer). Diana's positive comments about the lawyer made John reconsider his own opinion about him. During the new interactions, the lawyer was better able to keep open contact with all members, and this approach helped dissipate some tension in the whole system.

The Aftermath

Paul's will

While there were some positive developments in their relationships among family members, none of them completely addressed Paul's concerns with John and his actions regarding the Family Business. In light of the succession planning with Sara, and the reduction of tensions with John as a result of that succession planning and other events, Paul decided that he would defer any action on the subject until some point on the future, which would conceivably be post-mortem. He turned to his lawyer, who suggested creating a testamentary trust. One portion of his stock in the Family Business would go to each of John and Diana, but a slightly larger portion would go to John. The third portion would go into the testamentary trust. The trustee of that trust would have the right to award shares representing control of Paul's shares to John if John demonstrated to the trustee's satisfaction that John was conducting himself and had conducted himself in the best interest of the Family Business. If not, the trustee could award all of the shares in the trust to Diana. His lawyer suggested that Paul provide that Diana could disclaim some or all of those shares, in the interest of her relationship with John. At the same time, Paul's will would provide the dossier which summarized the evidence of John's past conduct regarding the Family Business to the trustee of that trust. At this point, Paul decided he would take no further action.

> ### *Insight:*
> *Relationship are characterized by reciprocity. This means that everybody plays a part in a given interaction and that the circular processes tends to continue over time. As revealed*

by the way Paul designed his testamentary trust, he thought that he needed to monitor and control the behavior of his "irresponsible" son, even after his death. He was not aware of how that belief fed into John's discomfort and promoted the very behavior Paul wanted to avoid. John, on the other hand, was not aware of how building a "secret escape route" from his "impossible" father, only gave him more reason to be suspicious of his behavior, perpetuating the distrust.

The tensions and potential for disconnects between Paul and John remained, even with the progress that had been made. Recently, Paul and John had an argument that stemmed from John not calling Paul on Father's Day, but only texting him instead. Several weeks later, Paul called John and made amends. John remarked by saying, "Don't worry, Dad, I won't ask you to apologize." Paul responded quickly: "Good, then I won't ask you to apologize for putting me through hell when you were arrested that night."

A few months later, Paul, his children, and grandchildren spent Thanksgiving together after a hiatus of several years.

Paul's lawyer came to have concerns over how the testamentary trust might operate in fact, and specifically whether it not only would produce benefits that were important to Paul, but also whether it would create other problems that were just as serious in magnitude as the ones it was designed to address. As the engagement ended, Paul was reconsidering what course to take regarding the trust.

There are threats to family harmony and functioning that remain for the Robertsons. Among these are the fact that the relationship between Paul and John is frayed and volatile and carries the potential for severe conflict that could spill over into and impact the Family Business. In some sense, both Paul and John attempt to control the other's behavior in a manner that is damaging to their relationship and the Family Business. Another is that the ineffective integration of Harold's family with Sara's family leads to tension, resentment, and occasional lack of communication and cooperation, all of which could damage the Family Business. Finally, the inclination of all parties to make important decisions that are emotionally-driven, rather than thoughtfully-driven, impacts their relationships and the Family Business.

Commentary on the Emotional Aspect of the Process

This case invites us to reflect upon four relevant elements in the practice of advising family businesses: a) Past family events impact relationships in the present (*Understanding the present in the light of the past*), b) Distance is a common reaction when tensions arise in a family, and it has predictable consequences (*Distance as a way to deal with tension in relationships*), c) As families grow and evolve they need to rethink and adjust their responsibility for self and to others (*Negotiating responsibilities*), and d) The advisor's management of self is key to the success of the engagement (*The professional as a resource to the family*).

Understanding the present in the light of the past

The lawyer's long-term engagement with the Robertsons provided a unique opportunity to obtain a detailed family history, with the added advantage of having the perspective of various family members. Learning about the history of a family goes beyond the anecdotal; it is paramount in guiding the professional's approach and interventions. In this case, knowing about the volatility between Paul and John and how their relationship evolved over time instructed the lawyer's style of engagement and communication. He was particularly careful in his interactions with Paul and John, making efforts to remain understated, patient, and nonjudgmental. Likewise, knowing the way Sara's family came to be part of the Robertson family helped him understand the raw emotions that were ever-present during the succession planning. This knowledge led him to take steps to minimize the impact of those emotions in the process of attaining an agreement which ultimately both Paul and Sara desired.

Getting the facts about the history of a family is a challenge for some advisors, particularly when the engagement is brief and narrow in focus. When the professional engagement is longer and larger in scope, there are more opportunities to regularly ask questions about the history and evolution of family relationships, and to refine the understanding of the family background. In this case the lawyer was consistently interested in knowing more about the family, but it took him some time before he got a more nuanced picture. For example, it was well into his work with this family that he learned about Paul's volatility as a father, which helped him understand John's relationship with his father more fully.

One common obstacle for acquiring a detailed and accurate family history is the sense that the advisor is overstepping the boundaries of his/her profession. This obstacle is usually overcome when the professional understands that knowing more about the client's family history, in fact, helps provide better service. Regardless of the type of engagement, good results are achieved if the advisor is capable of communicating that his/her knowledge of he family history will help advance the family's interest.

There is no doubt that professionals benefit from learning about the family history, but the family also draws a benefit from the process. It is well known that exploring one's own history provides an opportunity to increase the understanding of one's own background, as well as to help explain the ways one approaches life in the present. In the practice of advising family businesses, the family's understanding of the current problem is often modified and enriched as the result of investigating their own past, which in turn leads them to envision new alternatives. In this case, as Paul and Diana described the history of how Diana became financially dependent on her father, and how Paul became overburdened by his sense of responsibility towards Diana, they became clear about the development of events. This exploration itself pointed at the most logical solution: Paul had to cut down the financial help he was providing, and Diana needed to become more financially independent. In this sense, being interested in hearing about the evolution of a family serves a double purpose: the advisor can tailor his/her interventions with more precision, and the family can benefit from a richer comprehension about themselves.

Distance as a way to dealing with tension in relationships

Embedded in the nature of relationships is the continuous negotiation of the "space" between people. In other words, people constantly adjust the degree of involvement with one another.

Sometimes individuals are comfortable with a relationship characterized by closeness, sometimes they require some distance. This continuous adjustment is described as the counterbalancing of the forces toward togetherness and individuality. Togetherness is necessary and can create a sense of well-being, but it can also result in tension between people. Individuality is useful and necessary, but it has its limits given that we are social beings and we need each other for survival. People vary in the degree to which they are capable of maintaining their own individuality while they relate to others. Typically, when one or more individuals become uncomfortable through the tension created by their involvement with each other, they create distance to gain stability. Again, families vary in the extent to which they need distance to sustain such balance. The Robertson family used a great deal of distance as a way to manage the tension created by togetherness.

There are many examples in this family of how generation after generation, distance was used as a regulating strategy. Harold's affair with Sara represents a way of using distance to deal with tensions in the marriage. Harold and Michael did not talk to each other for more than a decade, and reportedly had a hard time being in the presence of each other. Margaret came across as an aloof and uninvolved mother. Paul, during his first years of semi-retirement, took so much distance from the Family Business that he almost lost contact with what was going on. Paul and Sara, the only two board members in the business, did not have meetings for years. John developed his own business as a way to create a space for himself and found it necessary to keep this information concealed from the family.

Business Problems and Family Problems Intertwined

Distance can alleviate the discomfort of the moment, but if it is sustained, it can create a new set of difficulties. The lack of contact contributes to the perception that the other is difficult, unreasonable, or uninterested. Distance also deepens emotional discomfort as it does not allow new interactions to put the past into perspective. In short, distance precludes knowing the other as a person and for the other to know one-self. The alternative is to actively engage with the distant party, face a problem, and discuss it as openly as possible.

Engaging in open discussions was new territory for the Robertson family. Steps taken in this direction included the agreement between Paul and Sara about succession planning, conversations about Diana's financial situation, discussions about balancing Paul's financial future, and conversations about the kind of support he wanted to offer to the next generation. Each step of the way the family was a little more capable of sustaining contact despite the disagreements or frictions. This capacity favored the attainment of the specific goals related to the projects assigned to the lawyer. Put differently, the family's increased capacity made it possible for the lawyer to deliver better services.

Negotiating responsibilities

All relationships require defining responsibilities. People are constantly erring and correcting between being overly responsible for someone or a situation, and functioning under one's capabilities, which means being less responsible for self. Some people, though, become "stuck" in one or the other position, referred to as an over/under-functioning pattern of relationship. For instance, Paul and Diana were fixed in a situation where Paul was financially supporting Diana well into her adult life (overstepping his fatherly responsibilities), while Diana financially relied on him despite her age and capabilities (not assuming responsibility for herself). This arrangement sustained their interdependence.

Over time, a relationship characterized by over/under functioning takes a toll on both parties. The person over-functioning is overburdened and exhausted, and the person under-functioning becomes helpless and frustrated. Both get irritated and angry, but they find it hard to change. Some life situations, such as Diana's financial crisis, represent an opportunity to challenge this pattern. In this case Paul and Diana responded with actions that led them into developing a more equal (adult-adult) relationship. In the process they re-negotiated what they conceived as their responsibilities for self and to each other. Paul decided he would no longer provide such large amounts of money to Diana and that he would focus on planning for his own future. Diana decided to get a job to bring income to her family and be more self-sufficient. It represented a step toward more maturity in the family, but one that would need time and sustained effort to consolidate.

Because families are systems, change in one individual affects other individuals and other relationships. In this case, the shift in the relationship between Paul and Diana had an effect on the relationship between Paul and John. As Paul and Diana reset their responsibilities, Paul and John saw theirs change as well. Paul lifted some pressure off John by making it unnecessary for him to deliver such large monthly distributions, in a sense he became less dependent on his son. John was relieved and could be more relaxed around his father, feeling less responsible for his well-being.

Business Problems and Family Problems Intertwined

It is necessary to realize that patterns established early in the life of a family are hard to change. In this family, the over/under-functioning pattern was firmly grounded, as observed in the following aspect of the father-son relationship: Paul was convinced that, to a certain extent, he could not trust John. This conviction was probably developed many years earlier and was crystalized when John hit a pedestrian while driving intoxicated. It is probable that Paul had not overcome the sense that he was responsible for containing his son's irresponsible behavior and in doing so he came across as controlling. John probably had the sense that his only option to gaining autonomy was by rebelling and breaking away from his father, coming across as uncommitted to the business, as well as unreliable.

This pattern was bound to continue even after Paul's death if Paul proceeded with the testamentary trust as he had structured it. The trust said that John would benefit only if he behaved in accordance with Paul's standards (through the evaluation of a trustee). This locked Paul in the over-functioning position. John reciprocated by continuing to grow his own company in secrecy as a way to "break free" from father. In this fashion he locked himself in the under-functioning position. As the lawyer became aware of the undesirable and unintended consequences of the design of the trust, he changed his ideas about the soundness of such structure and began to share them with Paul, who, by the time of this report, had begun to consider the downside of the approach he had taken.

It remains to be seen whether the members of this family can find the right level of responsibility for self while also sustaining the right level of responsibility to the group. The goal would be to find a way to relate to each other as adults, each looking after him/herself, while collaborating to strengthen both the Family Business and the family.

The professional as a resource to the family

A professional that can stay the course with a family as they move into the future adds value to that family. It is worth noting that in order to be a resource to the family, the advisor's most important tool is the person of the advisor him/herself, and his/her own level of maturity, also referred to as differentiation of self. That includes the capacity to maintain his/her thinking as clearly as possible while in the middle of an emotionally charged exchange. In other words, the advisor needs to be in good contact with the family, engaged and interested, yet maintain his/her own independent point of view.

In the present case there were various instances that illustrate this capacity in the lawyer. For example, it would have been easy for him to join Paul in his view of his son as an unpredictable individual who wasn't fully committed to the Family Business, as he did at the onset of the engagement. But the lawyer worked on developing his own opinion rather than accepting somebody else's assessment. This effort allowed him to connect with both father and son, appreciate their perspectives, and not lose sight of how each of them were part of the problem and could be part of the solution. The lawyer's neutrality allowed both father and son to adjust their perceptions of each other, which in turn freed them to be more trusting and collaborative.

Business Problems and Family Problems Intertwined

Another example of the lawyer maintaining his independent point of view in the middle of an emotionally charged exchange is the following: The night before finalizing the succession agreement between Paul and Sara, Paul became upset about one aspect of the agreement and wanted to back away from the whole plan. He called the lawyer, instructing him to cancel the deal. The lawyer listened to Paul's arguments but understood Paul's position to be motivated entirely by the emotion of the moment. Paul's desired action flatly contradicted what he had said in the past was his best interest. Despite Paul's insistence and distress, the lawyer did not agree with him. He reminded Paul of the reasons that led Paul to previously favor the agreement, and the costs if he did not go through with it. The lawyer was firm in his communications with Paul, knowing that Paul could fire him on the spot for what might be seen as insubordination. At the end of the conversation, the lawyer communicated that ultimately it was Paul's decision how to proceed but was vocal about his own opinion. Being able to regulate his own reactions in the heat of the conversation (i.e. not giving in into Paul's demands, but not imposing his own ideas either) helped Paul re-think his position and reconsider from a more dispassionate stance.

In the process of professional engagements, the family is transformed and the professional also develops. In hindsight, the lawyer acknowledged some of his interventions were very effective but some were not. As his involvement with the family developed, he became better able to understand the emotional factors that constantly operate in families, and act accordingly. For example, early in the engagement, he approached John in a somewhat adversarial fashion because he had identified too closely with

Paul's interpretation of the problem. His demeanor was correctly interpreted by John as a hostile escalation by Paul. Later on, he had to undo some of the damage he created with that initial approach. Another example is the recommendation of the testamentary trust. The lawyer came to have a more expansive view of how that trust could negatively impact the family and the business and began a new conversation with Paul. As the lawyer's work with this family progressed, he increased his capacity to maintain an independent posture from that of his client. He understood that, even when he was retained by one person, he needed to keep his own perspective for the ultimate benefit of Paul and Paul's interests.

Final Comments

There are threats to family harmony and functioning that remain for the Robertsons. Among these are the fact that the relationship between Paul and John is frayed and volatile and carries the potential for severe conflict that could spill over into and impact the Family Business. In some sense, both Paul and John attempt to control the other's behavior in a manner that is damaging to their relationship and the Family Business. Another is that the ineffective integration of Harold's family with Sara's family leads to tension, resentment, and occasional lack of communication and cooperation, all of which could damage the Family Business. Finally, the inclination of all parties to make important decisions that are emotionally-driven, rather than thoughtfully-driven, impacts their relationships and the Family Business.

Notwithstanding the tensions and potential for disconnects between Paul and John that remained, progress had been made.

Business Problems and Family Problems Intertwined

Recently, Paul and John had an argument that stemmed from John not calling Paul on Father's Day, but only texting him instead. Several weeks later, Paul called John and made amends. John remarked by saying, "Don't worry, Dad, I won't ask you to apologize." Paul responded quickly: "Good, then I won't ask you to apologize for putting me through hell when you were arrested that night."

A few months later, Paul, his children, and grandchildren spent Thanksgiving together after a hiatus of several years.

Lessons Learned

This case highlights three aspects of family dynamics that are universal to all families and relevant to family businesses: First, stressful events in the life of a family create a tense emotional climate that can persist for decades and even across generations. This in turn can have a detrimental impact on a family business. In this case, the way grandfather Harold handled his marital discontent created problems in the Family Business that persisted half a century later, when future generations were dealing with the succession of the business. Knowing about these past events clarified much about the present problems.

Second, professionals can play a significant role in stabilizing a family. In this case, the lawyer's participation over the course of a dozen years increased the family's capacity to address difficult matters. It may have made the difference between the Robertson family being torn apart by expensive and destructive litigation, and a family that, while beset by many complex problems, was still capable of enjoying time together with an intact business.

Third, families in business are a complex puzzle where problems and conflicts are never completely solved, and families are always vulnerable to repeating the patterns of the past. Paul's proposed disposition of his stock in the Family Business might seem reasonable now, but if implemented may reproduce in the future a variation of the same problem he is trying to solve in the present. Nevertheless, with professional intervention and through addressing a few issues at a time, the family can build up capacity based on their struggles and their successes. The steady progress towards greater emotional maturity gives the family a better chance for successfully maintaining their business, their wealth, and most importantly, the family unit.

Key Takeaways

- Explore the family history. Past events in the family illuminate the nature of present difficulties.

- Contact as many family members as possible. A richer family history is gathered by engaging with as many family members as possible.

- Work on improving yourself. The professional's personal development and increased maturity represents the most valuable resource he/she can offer to the family.

- Be realistic about possible changes. Relationship patterns are long-standing and difficult to alter, but they can be tamed down.

CHAPTER 5

THE SCIENCE BEHIND THE ANALYSIS: BOWEN FAMILY SYSTEMS THEORY

Each or the first four chapters presented a case that represent actual engagements with different degrees of success. A more consistent application of systems thinking would have improved the prospects for better outcomes. In the following pages, you'll find a discussion of Bowen family systems theory and other scientific facts about family functioning that will help in your engagements with families.

Bowen Family Systems Theory

Bowen family systems theory is the body of knowledge resulting from decades of research on the human family and how it operates. Based on systems thinking, and on facts about evolution, it offers a unique blueprint for understanding and improving human relationships. The theory, which is also referred to as Natural family systems theory (or Bowen theory), was introduced by Dr. Murray Bowen in the 1960s and has continued to develop and expand, attracting the attention of scientists, clinicians, family enterprise advisors, clergy, nurses, and many other professionals that work with families worldwide. The description of the theory presented here covers the concepts that are most relevant for family enterprise advisors.

The Family as a System

Some describe the family as the sum of individuals, but in reality, a family is much more than that. A family is an organism formed by interdependent parts. Just as the body is an organism that depends on the coordinated functioning of its parts, the family is a system comprised by individuals that are coordinated to ensure the survival of the group. Each and every individual in the family influences and is influenced by other members to different degrees.

Families are tied together by emotional bonds in a way that is akin to a mobile where each piece is directly or indirectly connected with the rest of the structure. In Dr. Bowen's words: "The family is a system in that a change in the functioning of one family member is automatically followed by a compensatory change in another family member."[1]

The family is also described as an "emotional unit." In this definition "emotional" refers to the innate forces that govern life, including not only human but any form of life, from the multicellular to complex social groups. In other words, families behave in predictable patterns, similar to an ant colony or a herd of elephants, that respond to instinctual forces that guide their behavior. But, in contrast to other species, humans have the unique advantage of being capable of modifying their behavior based on deliberation. This capacity is what we call intellect, which includes reflection, reason, and judgment. Interestingly enough, observations indicate that individuals and families more often act automatically, governed by emotional forces rather than by choice emerging from the intellect.

An example of automatic behavior in families is the following: when an important member declines in health or dies, the surviving members assume the functions this person used to perform. For instance, in a family where the mother functioned as the link between the siblings by receiving and distributing information, upon her death and after a period of relative disorganization, the oldest daughter becomes the new hub of information. This accommodation doesn't happen in a deliberate fashion, rather, it emerges spontaneously, representing the automatic response of the system to change.

Interdependency

Families are characterized by the interdependence of its members, that is, the fact that family members depend on each other for life sustaining functions and for energy efficiency. A sick husband cared for by his wife is an example of depending on other for survival. A family coming together to buy a family group health insurance to lower costs is an example of an interdependence that helps the group optimize the use of their resources.

Interdependence also refers to the fact that functioning in one individual in the family is contingent on the functioning of other individuals. For instance, it is widely known that if a mother is calm and confident the child will be at ease. Interdependence is powerful and can have an impact even at a physical level. For example, the case of a couple where one spouse is overwhelmed by life demands, but the other develops migraines for no apparent reason. The well-being of one individual is dependent on the well-being of other individuals in the group.

How exactly does this interdependence develop? How do family members influence each other at such a deep level? The answer lies in the mechanisms by which families organize to ensure the continuity of the group generation after generation. The human infant is born in total dependency to the parents to whom she develops a deep attachment. But it is not only the child who attaches to parents, parents and other family members also develop an attachment to the child. The strong mutual attachment results in heightened sensitivity to one another, such that they become capable of registering subtle changes in each other's levels of distress and/or pleasure.

For instance, we detect alterations in each other's gaze, movements, tone of voice, skin coloration, and facial expressions. We even react to what we believe others are thinking or feeling. A woman described how she was able to tell when her father was either pleased or displeased with the investment recommendations made by the financial advisor by a minuscule difference in the way he raised his nose. That tiny piece of information determined whether she'd be relaxed or tense in the meeting. This influenced her agreement or disagreement with the advisor. Family members are exquisitely attuned to one another and react so quickly that it usually happens without awareness.

The interdependence between family members can be observed at all levels, from the biological, to the emotional, psychological, and ideological. We are more interconnected than we realize, and the depth of the influence we exert on each other is profound. Nevertheless, not all families present the same degree of interdependence. The notion of variation in levels of interdependence will be further explained when we introduce the term "differentiation of self."

Reciprocity

Reciprocity is a characteristic of the family system. People tend to take a contrary position to another in the group, similar to a seesaw effect. For example, the more a brother is focused on making money, the more the sister is uninterested in creating wealth. It is impossible to identify the origin of a reciprocal interaction, but it is equally important to recognize that, at any given time, each family member influences and is influenced by others in a dynamic fashion.

People also tend to assume complementary relationship postures that counterbalance each other's position. For instance, the more one parent is strict and rigid with the children, the more the other is lax and permissive. The more extreme the position of one individual, the more intense the response in the opposite direction of the other. When one individual moves toward "the center," the other is less compelled to take an extreme stance. Reciprocity can also be activated in a non-antagonistic fashion. The generosity of one person can result in others responding with generosity.

Circular interactions (or "circular causality") is a form of reciprocity. It refers to the fact that A responds to B, and that such response has an effect on B who responds to A. For example, a wife acts disappointed with her husband. Her husband responds by getting upset, the wife distances herself because she does not want to be with an upset husband, so he becomes furious with the wife for moving away. This chain of reactions can escalate to intense conflict until something happens that triggers the de-escalation, which represents the same phenomena in the opposite direction. "Any one significant family member who can "cool" the anxious response, or control one's own anxiety, can make steps toward de-escalation."[2]

Another form of reciprocity is the tendency to over/under function. That is, to take more or less responsibility than required for someone in a specific role. In other words, the over adequacy of one emerges as a response to the inadequacy of the other and vice-versa. When one member of the family fails to perform, there is a tendency for someone else to take on the responsibility. For instance, when a mother ceases caring for the young, another family member, say a daughter, takes on the responsibility. The more daughter takes charge, the more mother falls into dysfunction. Taking on responsibilities that do not correspond to someone's role is adaptive under certain circumstances, for example, when someone is temporarily sick. Yet, when this over/under functioning becomes fixed, it creates a new set of problems. In the prior example, the daughter might grow resentful for the many obligations she had to assume at an early age, the siblings may get annoyed and hostile towards the sister who they experience as bossy, and mother might become helpless.

The extent of reciprocal interactions and interdependency in a family group reveals the level of maturity of the group. More mature families are less inclined to lead their interactions in a reciprocal fashion and consequently members are more autonomous. More mature individuals can take positions that are less determined by the other and more self-defined.

Awareness of the reality of reciprocity helps one to take a neutral stance when observing a family interaction. It favors an appreciation of how interactions unfold over time, and it avoids falling into seeing "angels and devils" or "victims and perpetrators." For example, for decades a husband has taken care of completing tax returns for the couple. The times when the wife showed interest he responded dismissively saying: "don't worry, I will take care of it." The wife was satisfied with the answer. At one point, the husband became overwhelmed by a downturn of the business and he neglected filing taxes for two consecutive years. They blamed each other. The husband was resentful for having taken the burden of the filing for years. The wife was angry for having been ignored in her desire to participate. The systems thinker knows that both played a part in the problem and that they are both embedded in an over/under functioning reciprocity.

It is fair to affirm that at any given situation everybody plays a part in a problem and everybody can play a part in solving it.

"Systems theory assumes that all important people in the family unit play a part in the way family members function in relation to each other and in the way the symptom finally erupts."[3]

Individuality and Togetherness

Bowen theory postulates that natural systems, the family being one, are under the influence of two opposing and counterbalancing life forces that govern relationships. One leads towards individuality. The other, equally strong, leads towards togetherness.[4] Humans constantly struggle to strike a balance between these two urges. We have an impetus towards being alone, autonomous, towards making our own choices and leading our lives based on personal beliefs and goals. Likewise, we are pulled towards being in relationship, form bonds and affiliations, seek approval, and to think, feel and do in accordance with the group.[5]

Each family unit deals differently with the tension created by the opposing forces of individuality and togetherness. Each finds a unique balance that is comfortable, yet this balance is never static but in dynamic equilibrium. Life circumstances at each developmental stage of the family require adjusting the degree to which life energy is directed towards relationships or directed towards self. Some situations, particularly anxious times, move families towards the togetherness end of the spectrum. As togetherness increases people experience a sense of belonging and completeness. The downside of togetherness is that, as boundaries are blurred and fusion increases, the capacity to follow one's own compass is compromised and group thinking—with its multiple limitations—emerges. Eventually togetherness becomes uncomfortable and tensions arise, sometimes pushing people to relationship aversion or to develop symptoms.

Observing the self and others moving between the poles of individuality and togetherness provides information about what is going on in the group. It gives clues about the level of anxiety present. It also signals the way individuals are assessing reality and making decisions. For example, a family board under high pressure will be less tolerant of diverse opinions, individuals will tend to find ways to be accepted, and they will tend to increase expectations for compliance and agreement. People will be more vulnerable to be influenced by other's opinion and they experience a greater urge to accommodate to the group's demands. This represents a group that has moved toward togetherness. On the contrary, a more relaxed family board encourages new initiatives, people show stronger convictions and feel more comfortable being true to their own principles. When there is room for more individuality there is more stability and more capacity for clear thinking.

Differentiation of Self

Differentiation of self is the cornerstone concept in Bowen theory. It refers to the degree of autonomy between family members. In other words, the degree to which family members regulate each other. This regulation between family members remains true even after children in a family become adults. Through time family members continue to depend on and regulate each other in many ways, from the emotional to the practical. They rely on each other for thinking, feeling, and doing. The influence exerted on each other goes from the biological to the behavioral and cultural.

Not all families have the same degree of dependency among its members. Some have more "fluid boundaries" and some have less permeable, better defined limits. There is great variation from family to family, from those comprised of members whose selves are fused with each other to families with members who have better defined identities. The concept of differentiation of self refers to this variation and to the fact that all families fall along a continuum from fusion to differentiation.

Why Does Differentiation of Self Matter?

Differentiation of self is a complex concept that can be equated to the idea of maturity. In more differentiated families there is more room for diversity, for members to have their own ideas and life projects. They are better able to cooperate and are less vulnerable to the ups and downs of life circumstances. Less differentiated families demand conformity, are more reactive to each other, and are more prone to all sorts of long-lasting problems. Members of a multigenerational family tend to have similar levels of differentiation of self, with small variations from person-to-person and from generation to generation.

Differentiation of self remains fairly stable throughout a person's lifetime. Nevertheless, an individual can increase his/her own level of differentiation, which can have profound effects on his/her life course. Small changes in levels of differentiation may result in quite dissimilar outcomes. For example, a slight shift represents the difference between two brothers prematurely selling their family business because they can't deal with each other, and them maintaining a viable relationship until circumstances are favorable for an advantageous sell. A small difference in levels of maturity brings about a big difference in results.

More mature families are better able to use their resources, grow, create, take advantage of opportunities, and withstand difficulties. They have better chances of continuing their family enterprise over generations. On the contrary, less mature families might have extreme success at one point in time but are more vulnerable to unfavorable circumstances and tend to have shorter-lived family enterprises.

A quality of more differentiated families is the capacity to allow for leadership to emerge and for such leadership to be effective. In a family that has attained greater levels of differentiation individuals have well-defined life goals for self and are capable of leading when necessary and letting others lead when appropriate. In this sense leadership comes from self and not from telling others what to do. Mature leaders have clarity about what they will and will not do, and about the principles guiding their decisions and behavior. Mature leaders also give room for others to grow and follow their own paths.

Differentiation requires energy, clarity, and determination. It is not an easy task. It is predictable that when a person makes a differentiating move, others in the family will react and demand that he/she change back. Yet, if this person is able to sustain the effort long enough, the rest of the family accepts the shift, usually appreciates it, and eventually they move up their functioning as well. When this happens, the family as a group has increased its capacity to adapt to life challenges.

The Biological Underpinnings of Differentiation of Self

Differentiation of self refers to the way an individual handles his/her relationships, that is in a more fused or more autonomous fashion. Such mode of relating, in turn, responds to the level of integration between the individual's emotional and intellectual systems. Neuroscience provides facts about brain development, architecture, and functioning, and about the stress system and other biological factors that support the concept of differentiation of self as the result of the individual's intermix between emotion and intellect.

Human development is shaped by the interaction between genes and environment. The family is the primary context where this interaction takes place, which gives the family a particularly relevant role in brain development. It is well established that the brain changes only marginally after the formative years, consequently experiences during infancy, childhood, and adolescence are determinant for learning abilities, behavior, self-regulation, and psychological functioning.[6]

The neuroscientist Paul McLain, in the 1960's[7] proposed a brain model comprised of three distinct layers with different functional domains, which he called the "triune brain" (three brains in one). Although newer neuroscientific discoveries provide a more nuanced description of the complexities of this organ, his early model is still a useful organizing metaphor of brain functions.[8]

The three brains described by McLain are (a) the reptilian, (b) the mammalian, and (c) the neo- cortex. (a) The oldest brain in

Business Problems and Family Problems Intertwined

evolutionary terms is the reptilian. It commands automatic, regulatory functions, for example the response of the body to a drop of temperature or a change in blood glucose (muscle shivering and hunger, respectively). (b) The second brain is the mammalian brain or limbic system, involved in emotions. It is also responsible for parental behavior including attachment, care for the young, and play. (c) The last brain to evolve is the neo-cortex. This is the part of the brain where thinking takes place and therefore language, abstraction, planning, and perception is possible. It is considered the headquarters of planning, focus, self-control, awareness, and flexibility. In reality the three brains are in constant communication and mutual regulation. In fact, an appropriate response to a given situation requires information, "cross—checking," and engagement of multiple parts of the brain simultaneously. Notwithstanding, intentional self-regulation (or "top-down regulation") implies that the neo-cortex is in charge.

In Bowen family systems theory terms, automatic or instinctual responses coming from any of the "three brains" is referred to as the emotional system. It goes from body functions and the experience of emotions, to the interpretation of environmental information. It determines things like where we direct our attention, or whether we approach or distance from others. The emotional system is very powerful and fast, therefore mostly working out of our awareness. In contrast the intellectual system is slow and requires more energy. It refers to functions such as reflection, analysis, goal direction, and thoughtfulness. The intellectual system receives information from the emotional system but is capable of overriding it in favor of behavior guided by deliberation. The Center on the

Developing Child at Harvard University calls this the "intentional self-regulation" which is our conscious and proactive response needed for achieving goals. It explains the human's capacity to make decisions that, despite momentary discomfort, yield better results in the long run. For example, "I feel like running away from this situation, but I know I have to address this topic with father, thus, I stay and have a conversation."

People vary in the degree to which these two systems are distinct but integrated, meaning the degree to which they are fused or differentiated. In the fused state, the emotional system "drives the bus" and the thinking is in the service of supporting it. In the differentiated state, the emotional system provides information, but the intellectual system determines the actions and direction in a coordinated fashion. As described by Bowen, "(a)t the fusion end of the spectrum, the intellect is so flooded by emotionality that the total life course is determined by the emotional process of what "feels right" rather than by beliefs or opinions. The intellect exists as an appendage of the feeling system."[9]

The Link Between Biology and Relationships

There is correspondence between the level of differentiation of the emotional and intellectual systems of an individual and his/her style of relating to others. When the emotional and intellectual systems are more fused people are also more fused with each other. Conversely, when the intellectual and the emotional systems are more distinct, the individual has more choices as to how to relate to others. For example, a father at higher levels of differentiation will come to the following conclusion: "I have an urge to give my daughter money and to protect her. It makes me happy to see her happy. But reality tells me that she is a professional woman, capable of earning her own money. I suspect that my gift will interfere with her efforts to becoming more autonomous." In this example the emotional system represents the desire of immediate gratification of father and his urge of protecting offspring, the intellectual system represents the assessment of reality and the awareness of the impact of his behavior on his daughter. The result is his ability to guide his behavior towards daughter in a more deliberate fashion and his ability to allow "space" between them.

In summary, differentiation between emotions and intellect and differentiation in relationships go hand in hand, and together represent the level of differentiation of self of an individual. Attaining greater levels of differentiation represent internal and external changes that go in tandem. That is, working on differentiation of self requires increased self-regulation as well as changes in the way one handles relationships. Best results are obtained when efforts at differentiating a self are exercised in real-life interactions with important others.

The Multigenerational Family

Family consultants guided by systems thinking give particular importance to understanding the multi-generational family history and connecting with the various generations. The human family evolved to live and raise their offspring in multigenerational groups giving it an advantage for adapting. This also means that any given nuclear family is influenced by what happened two, three, four, and more generations before. As a way of example, looking closely at the history of a family that owns a business, one can identify evidence of an entrepreneurial mindset already present in previous generations. One can also track ways in which the family has dealt with business initiatives and connect it to the way the family is responding in the present. The influence of what happened in previous generations is manifested at many levels including in our biology, our relationship patterns, and our family culture.

Family systems theory has identified advantages implicit in maintaining fluid contact with previous generations. The degree of contact a person has with his parental and extended family (grandparents, parents, aunts and uncles, and cousins) and knowledge about facts pertaining to his family going back several generations, is associated with more stability over his lifetime. Contact with the extended family is also associated with fewer symptoms and better family functioning.[10]

Families vary in the degree to which its members maintain contact with previous generations. It ranges from those who know their history and are in viable contact with most of their family members, to those who live their life in isolation from their own kin. The extreme version of denying the connection to previous generations is called "cutoff." Cutoff can be manifested in emotional disconnect (interpersonal barriers that inhibit open communication) and/or in geographical distance.

Cutoffs emerge from the difficulties people have in sustaining relationships with family members. It responds to the way they are affected by contact, sometimes going as far as to create dysfunction such as depression, health problems, and stress. A man declared his determination to stay away from his family because he said his family was "toxic" and they "made him sick." His family preferred him away because, they said, "he is impossible to be around" and "he disrupts the family peace."

Cutoff is an emotional reaction, namely an automatic or instinctive response to the inability to deal with the anxiety resulting from the intensity of certain relationships. Cutoff is different from leaving the family to pursue one's own life goals. The problem with cutoff is that the intensity the person is running away from is replicated in new relationships. A version of the problem is repeated in current relationships and with future generations as exemplified by the following situation: a brother interrupted contact with his family of origin after disagreements about the way wealth was transferred from his parents to him and his siblings. The brother created a tightly knit nuclear family that was severed years later because a daughter disagreed with her parents and siblings about the handling of the business. Unintentionally, the inability of the first generation to deal with each other and their differences resulted in the repetition of the emotional intensity and then disconnect, between family members in the next generation. This is the nature of cutoff.

Anxiety In the System

Bowen family systems theory has a unique way of understanding anxiety and the impact it has on individual functioning, family interactions, and multigenerational processes. In a nutshell, anxiety is an organism's response to perceived threat, whether it is real or imagined. Acute anxiety is related to present time—real threats (for example, losing a home) and chronic anxiety is related to anticipation of a threat (for example, "mother might develop cancer in her 40s as grandmother did"). Usually acute anxiety is shorter lived, and chronic anxiety is sustained over longer periods of time, even across generations.

The presence of anxiety over extended periods of time makes it more difficult to detect because such state of arousal is experienced as normal. Chronic anxiety is transmitted from generation to generation and it is embedded in the individual's biology, psychology, and culture. For example, a traumatic loss of wealth due to a social revolution had ripple effects two generations down in the shape of some members taking the attitude of "spend and enjoy wealth while it lasts" and others having attitudes such as "it is not worth working for a goal if gains will be lost anyway." Neither attitude towards wealth was based on the present financial reality of the family, rather each seemed to be a response to the past experience.

Chronic anxiety becomes "the air a family breathes" and might not be evident until the family faces a particular stressful situation. In those instances, the family might be less able to adapt and might be more prone to fall into dysfunction. Chronic anxiety renders the family group less flexible and more sensitive to certain situations, as well as more reactive. Bowen describes: "[W]hen a family is subjected to chronic, sustained anxiety, the family begins to lose contact with its intellectually determined principles, and to resort more and more to emotionally determined decisions to allay the anxiety of the moment. The results of the process are symptoms and eventually regression to a lower level of functioning."[11]

Business Problems and Family Problems Intertwined

When the stress response is activated, most people use a set of behavioral responses. Typical behaviors of anxious people include attacking, distancing or fleeing, being vigilant, becoming defensive, being protective, blaming others, and scapegoating. Anxiety travels quickly in families in an infectious fashion. Being with an anxious person makes anybody feel uneasy quite rapidly. Depending on the family's way of reacting to threatening situations, anxiety can be transmitted and amplified, or neutralized and dissipated.

One of the hallmarks of anxiety is that it compromises clear thinking. This is a well-established fact, as explained by the neuroscientist Daniel Levitin from McGill University. He states that the brain under stress:

> "releases cortisol, increases your heart rate, modulates adrenalin levels and it clouds your thinking. [O]ur brain under stress releases cortisol, and one of the things that happens at that moment is that a whole bunch of systems shut down. There's an evolutionary reason for this. In face-to-face with a predator, you don't need your digestive system, or your libido, or your immune system, because if your body is expending metabolism on those things and you don't react quickly, you might become the lion's lunch, and then none of those things matter. Unfortunately, one of the things that goes out the window during those times of stress is rational, logical thinking."[12]

When people are anxious, the capacity to activate the intellectual system is compromised. In those instances, the emotional system, for example the fight/flight response, takes over and thinking is inhibited. Lowering the anxiety permits the re-activation of the intellectual system allowing for more realistic assessment of situations, the capacity of seeing new options, flexibility, and the ability to engage with others in productive ways. From this fact stems the importance of lowering of anxiety when important conversations are held and decisions are made, as indicated by family consultation guided by Bowen theory. It is important to note that at higher levels of differentiation, individuals have greater ability to sustain thinking in the midsts of anxiety.

Relationship Patterns and Anxiety

Bowen theory identifies four ways in which nuclear families deal with the anxiety that emerges from the tension, demands, frictions, and expectations that are part of everyday family life. The four patterns are a) distance, b) conflict in the marriage, c) dysfunction in a spouse, d) projection onto a child and impairment in that child. None of these patterns are intentional; rather, they happen in an automatic fashion and represent mechanisms families use to attempt to adapt to life challenges.

Some families deal with difficulties through distancing. They might move away from each other through divorce, immigration, going quiet, or interrupting all communications. In other families the problems are expressed in the marriage through bickering, conflict, and even violence. In some families it is one member of the couple whose functioning is compromised by problems such as physical symptoms, emotional symptoms, or irresponsible behavior. Finally, other families focus intensely on children, both on their attainments and on their problems, and these children, who

Business Problems and Family Problems Intertwined

absorb a disproportionately large amount of family anxiety, tend to develop more problems in life (physical, emotional and social symptoms). Some families use all patterns and some use one or two in a more fixed way.

Typically, the exploration of the multigenerational family reveals that for generations, families use similar mechanism over and over. By way of an example, consider the following family presenting the pattern "dysfunction in a spouse." The wife was depressed and abused alcohol while the husband was a successful business person, well respected in the community, and took care of all administrative aspects of the home. A closer look at the family history showed that grandmother and grandfather also functioned in the same way (one being overly adequate and the other inadequate), and that in the extended family there were several cases where one spouse ended up taking care of the sick/incapable/weak partner. Emotional patterns are typically replicated over generations.

The relationship patterns have the double effect of in the short run releasing some of the anxiety accumulated in the system, and in the long run creating more problems and thus increasing the chronic anxiety of the unit. In this sense, these mechanisms are considered to be useful up to a point but are inadequate adaptive strategies when they become fixed and long-standing.

Triangles

The discovery of the relationship triangle is one of the most important concepts introduced by Bowen theory, and it opened new avenues to conceptualizing relationships. When one thinks about relationships, usually a two-person interaction comes to mind. In reality, a two-person relationship is relatively unstable and the introduction of a third person brings stability. A third person can be brought in by thinking or talking about him/her or through his/her physical presence. A direct conversation about "me and you" does not last long before the attention is diverted onto a third party. Dr. Bowen described the triangle as the basic building block of relationships. Triangles are so basic and automatic that they can be observed not only in the human family but also in other forms of life. In this sense, forming triangles emerges from the emotional system.

Triangles are formed by two people who agree with each other (the insiders) and one who disagrees or who is more distant (the outsider). These positions can be fixed or flexible. When they are flexible one is the outsider and the next moment, he/she is the insider only to move back to the outside position in a short period of time.

Triangles are neither good nor bad, they just are. They have the potential to amplify anxiety and to create problems. They also have the potential to contain anxiety, and be adaptive and constructive. In this sense they have the potential to be useful. The key to useful triangles lies in the capacity of one of the players to stay in equal contact with the other two angles of the triangle, and to be able to direct the problem back to where it originally belonged. It also requires the third person to remain in contact with the two others as directly as possible. For example, if a daughter is complaining to her mother about her annoying husband, she can either join the daughter in her view of the husband as difficult, feel sorry for her daughter and be cold with the son-in-law, or she can say something to the effect of "it sounds like this is something important you have to talk about with your husband" and continue a conversation about a different topic. Equally important is for her to continue treating her son-in-law in the same friendly manner as before.

Triangles are a natural way of dealing with tension. When a triangle cannot contain any more tension, a series of interlocking triangles emerge. Maneuvering in interlocking triangles can be tricky, yet, if someone in the system is able to see the triangles and track their movements, it gives him an advantage and allows him to be more intentional in the way he communicates and behaves.

Understanding triangles is particularly important for family advisors who are inherently "triangled in" as clients work their way through decision-making. For these advisors, the best way to learn about triangles and how to manage self within them is through observing and intervening in triangles in their own families. Especially important is the primary triangle (the most influential triangle in a person's life) formed by father, mother, and self. There is no shortage of opportunities in a person's life to observe and test triangles.

Sibling Position

What makes each of us similar and different from our siblings? How to account for differences in siblings who were all born and raised in the same family? Sibling position is a crucial variable, albeit not the only one, that helps answer these questions.

Walter Toman[13] a German psychiatrist who was a contemporary of Dr. Bowen, provided invaluable information about the sibling group and the connection between sibling position and personality. By studying sibling position, he was able to identify characteristics that emerge from being the younger brother of brothers, the younger sister of brothers, the younger brother of sisters, etc. He outlined 10 different sibling positions and their typical characteristics. He also noted factors that shift the typical profiles. Factors such as losses in the family, the ages between siblings, special events such as illness or disabilities in a sibling, are a few examples.

Information about sibling position helps understand adult behavior, including how people handle their marriage, and how they make important decisions. Facts about sibling position are so important that Dr. Bowen noted: "[B]ased on my research and therapy, I believe that no single piece of data is more important than knowing the sibling position of people in the present and past generations."[14]

Observations and facts about the sibling position and the particularities of specific family constellations has continued to be investigated given its relevance to family functioning by authors such as Berthoud,[15] Lamb & Sutton-Smith,[16] Leman,[17] and Sulloway.[18] Understanding this dynamic is crucial for family advisors when dealing with themes such as succession or sibling shared decision-making. It reveals an underlying system of relationships that is usually established in childhood, and which typically remains true throughout later years. Knowing about sibling position and its effects also provides insight into how siblings can adjust their interactions to promote higher levels of collaboration.

Events Shaping the Multigenerational Family

There are many factors, other than sibling position, that shape the family environment where an individual develops. Of particular importance are births, deaths, marriages, divorces and migration. Such context is key for the "emotional programming" that takes place during the growing up years, which largely determines the way people engage with the world later in life. Characteristics such as the inclination to take responsibility or accommodate, be other-centered or self-centered, be more or less reactive to feeling states in self and in others, be more complaint or more rebellious, and the degree of sensitivity to potential danger or to criticism, are tendencies that are developed early in life in response to a specific family context.

The impact of certain events in the family history affect not only the present but transcends generations. For example, a mother who dies in childbirth leaving a father widowed with children has short-term and long-term implications. The event impacts the kind of relationship father has with each child. The absence of the mother might invite a more active participation of the paternal grandparents in child-rearing and more distance from the maternal family. Some children, depending on their developmental stage at the time of their mother's death, will absorb more or less the family's grief and possibly be more apprehensive at the time of the birth of their own children. An event such as this one has a powerful "wave shock effect." Being aware of past events and people's reactions to those events is useful for understanding a family with its strengths and shortcomings.

The Professional and the Client Family

A professional working with a family, to a greater or lesser degree, becomes part of the family's relationship system. They are as vulnerable as the family members to being affected by the anxiety in the system and to being drawn into the interlocking triangles. Likewise, the professional, being part of the system, has the potential to intervene in a way that favors the system and increases its capacity to face challenges in the most mature way possible.

Professionals working with families are better equipped if they can accomplish a double task: one that has to do with knowing and another that has to do with being. Knowing refers to obtaining proficiency in their own field of expertise. Knowing also refers to being cognizant about family dynamics and human relationships. Being refers to the capacity of engaging in relationships and in developing interest in the client family while maintaining appropriate boundaries. Being has also to do with assuming responsibility without being overly responsible. Lastly, being links to an understanding of oneself, having the capacity to self-regulate, and the ability to sustain thinking in the midst of anxiety. In one sentence, being represents constant work on differentiation of self.

SOURCES

(1) Bowen, M. (1978) *Family Therapy in Clinical Practice.* London, New York: NY: Jason Aronson, pp.260.

(2) Idem, pp.267.

(3) Idem, pp.260.

(4) Bowen, M., Kerr, M. (1988) *Family Evaluation. An Approach Based on Bowen Theory.* New York, London: Norton.

(5) Gilbert, R. (1992) *Extraordinary Relationships. A New Way of Thinking About Human Interactions.* New York: John Wiley & Sons.

(6) Center on the Developing Child at Harvard University (2016) Building Core Capabilities for Life: the Science Behind the Skills Adults Need to Succeed in Parenting and the Workplace. Retrieved from *https://developingchild.harvard.edu/resources/building-core-capabilities-for-life/*. Accessed on April 1, 2019.

(7) McLean, P. (1990) *The Triune Brain in Evolution. Role in Paleocerebral Functions.* New York: Plenum Press.

(8) Sapolski, R. (2017) *Behave. The Biology of Humans at Our Best and Our Worst.* New York, NY: Penguin Press.

(9) Bowen, M. (1978) *Family Therapy in Clinical Practice.* London, New York: NY: Jason Aronson, pp.263.

(10) Klever, P. (2015) Multigenerational Relationship and Nuclear Family Functioning. *The American Journal of Family Therapy* 43: 339-351.

(11) Bowen, M. (1978) *Family Therapy in Clinical Practice.* London, New York: NY: Jason Aronson, pp.386.

(12) Levitin, D. (2015, October) Daniel Levitin: How to stay calm when you know you'll be stressed [Video file]. Retrieved from *https://www.ted.com/talks/daniel_levitin_how_to_stay_calm_when_you_know_you_ll_be_stressed*. Accessed on April 1, 2018.

(13) Toman, W. (1993) *Family Constellation. Its Effects on Personality and Social Behavior.* 4th Ed. New York, NY: Springer Publishing Company.

(14) Bowen, M. (1978) *Family Therapy in Clinical Practice.* London, New York: NY: Jason Aronson, pp.385.

(15) Berthoud, J. (1996) *Pecking Order. How Your Place in the Family Affects Your Personality.* London: Victor Gollancz.

(16) Lamb, E., Sutton-Smith, B. (Eds.) (1982) *Sibling Relationships: Their Nature and Significance Across the Lifespan.* Hillsdale, NJ, London: Lawrence Erlbaum Associates, Publishers.

(17) Leman, K. (2009) *The Birth Order. Why You Are the Way You Are.* Grand Rapids, Michigan: Revell.

(18) Sulloway, F. (1996) *Born to Rebel. Birth Order, Family Dynamics, and Creative lives.* New York, NY: Pantheon Books.

Made in the USA
Columbia, SC
23 September 2019